AF292112

OUR WORLD in NUMBERS

PLANET EARTH

AN ENCYCLOPEDIA OF FANTASTIC FACTS

1,100 CUBIC M
83 species
17 gigawatts
965 KPH
6.1 hectares
£36.2 million
1—2 G
5 seconds
78%
16,350 KM
400 tonnes
2.4 litres
58 times

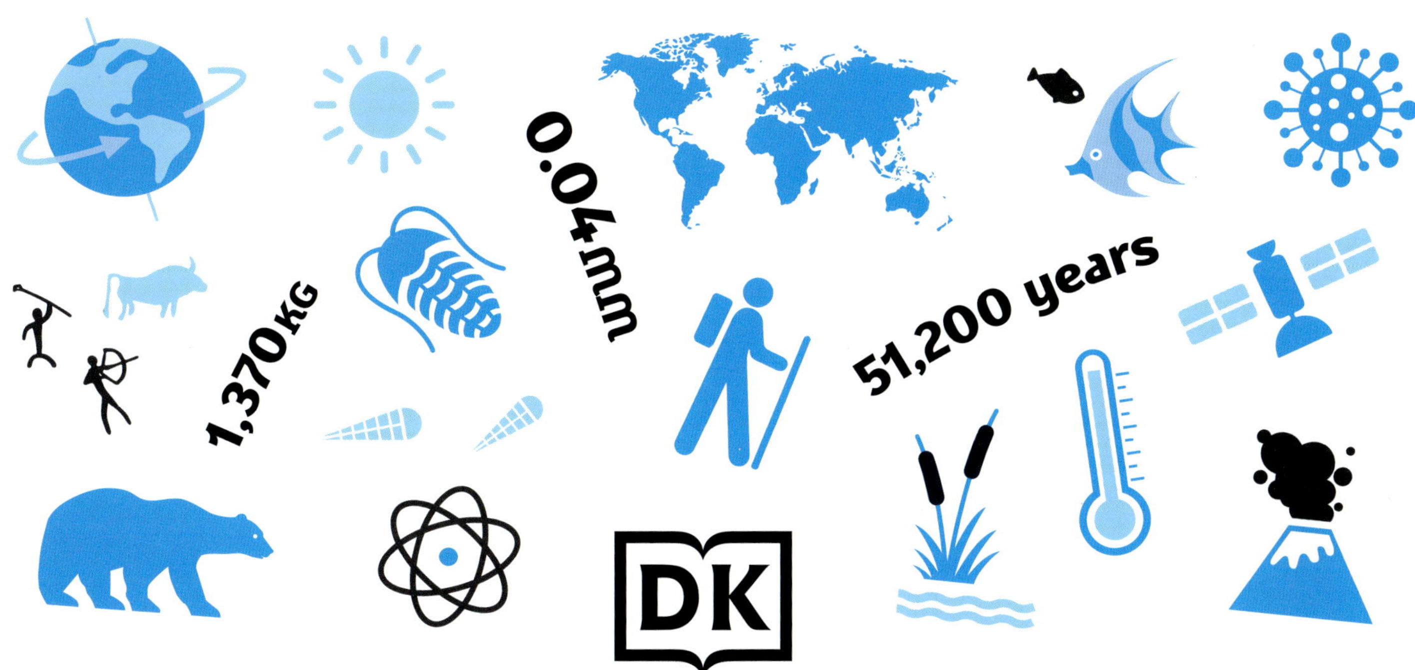

DK

PLANET EARTH

AN ENCYCLOPEDIA OF FANTASTIC FACTS

Written by
WILLIAM POTTER, ALICIA WILLIAMSON, AND RICHARD MEAD

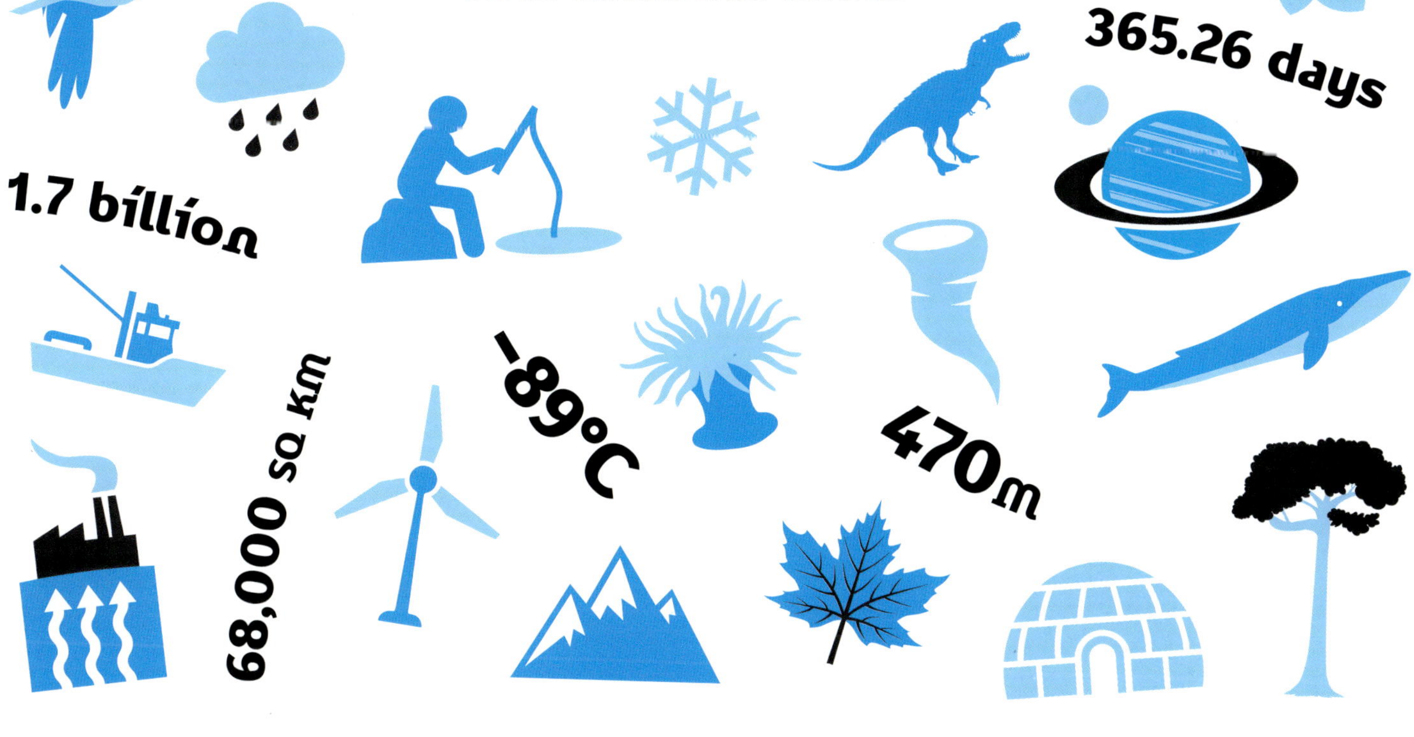

CONTENTS

Produced for DK by
Dynamo Limited
1 Cathedral Court, Southernhay East, Exeter EX1 1AF

Editorial Partner Alicia Williamson
Design Partner Jeremy Marshall
Expert Consultant Philip Eales

Project Editor Jolyon Goddard
Senior Art Editor Jacqui Swan
Managing Editor Rachel Fox
Managing Art Editor Owen Peyton Jones
Production Editor Becky Fallowfield
Production Controller Ben Radley
Jacket Designer Vidushi Chaudhry
DTP Designer Rakesh Kumar
Art Director Mabel Chan
Publisher Andrew Macintyre

First published in Great Britain in 2025 by
Dorling Kindersley Limited
20 Vauxhall Bridge Road,
London SW1V 2SA

The authorised representative in the EEA is
Dorling Kindersley Verlag GmbH. Arnulfstr. 124,
80636 Munich, Germany

Copyright © 2025 Dorling Kindersley Limited
A Penguin Random House Company
10 9 8 7 6 5 4 3 2 1
001-349315-May/2025

A CIP catalogue record for this book
is available from the British Library.
ISBN: 978-0-2417-3863-4

Printed and bound in China

www.dk.com

MIX
Paper | Supporting
responsible forestry
FSC™ C018179

This book was made with Forest
Stewardship Council™ certified
paper – one small step in DK's
commitment to a sustainable future.
Learn more at **www.dk.com/uk/
information/sustainability**

BLUE PLANET

LIVING PLANET

CHANGING PLANET

HUMAN PLANET

NOTE: THE FACTS AND STATISTICS IN THIS BOOK WERE CORRECT AT THE TIME OF GOING TO PRESS.

OUR PLANET IN NUMBERS

We live in a world of numbers. Measurements and calculations help us learn more about the planet we live on. They can tell us about Earth's 4.54 billion years of history and what might happen to it in the future. Throughout this book, you'll read facts and answer questions like the ones below, and many more.

How **OLD** is Earth's crust?

How do we know the age of things that are millions of years older than us? Earth is covered with layers of rock that have built up slowly over time. Each layer corresponds to a specific period in the planet's history. Rocks can be dated by measuring their radioactive elements or magnetic properties.

How **FAR** away is the Moon?

Distances on Earth are often measured in mm (millimetres), cm (centimetres), and km (kilometres). We can now precisely calculate very large distances – such as the 384,400km to our Moon – by figuring out how long it takes a radio signal to travel to and from a location.

How **BIG** is the biggest lake?

The size of something can be measured in different ways. A lake's size can be calculated by its length and width in km (kilometres), surface area in sq km (square kilometres), or volume in cubic km (cubic kilometres).

How **DEEP** is the ocean?

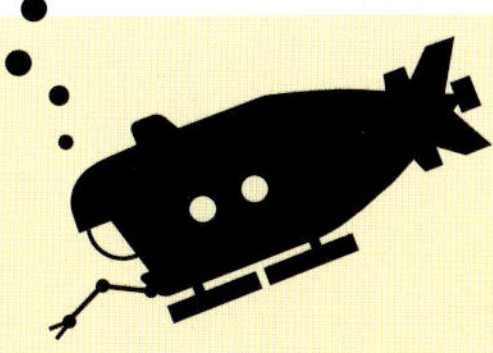

Heights and depths on Earth are usually measured according to how far above or below sea level (the average height of the ocean's surface) they are.

How **FAST** does a tornado spin?

Speed, most often clocked in kph (kilometres per hour), can tell us how fast something is moving. There are many methods and instruments for measuring speed. In the case of a tornado, experts can analyse radar echoes and the destruction it causes.

How **COLD** is the coldest place?

We compare how hot or cold a place or thing is by gauging its temperature according to a set scale. In the Celsius scale, 0°C is the freezing point (and 100°C is the boiling point) of water under normal conditions.

How **MANY** people live in the biggest city?

"How many?" is not always a simple matter of counting. Population, for instance, is sometimes based on an official census (count) and sometimes on estimates created by data scientists. Today, counting geographic features such as islands is much easier with satellite imaging, but you still have to agree on what counts as an island first!

THIRD PLANET FROM THE SUN

Exceptional
EARTH

Our one-of-a-kind planet, the third closest to the Sun, has all the right ingredients for life – light and warmth from the Sun, abundant liquid water, and a breathable atmosphere that traps in heat. It is home to more than 8 million animal and plant species, including over 8.1 billion people.

EARTH is estimated to be **4.54 BILLION YEARS OLD,** less than **1/3** the **AGE OF THE UNIVERSE.**

Earth is the **fifth- LARGEST PLANET** in the **Solar System.**

ONE EARTH DAY (the time it takes our planet to spin around **ONCE** on its axis) is **23.9 HOURS.**

The **oceans** cover around **70.8%** of **EARTH'S SURFACE.**

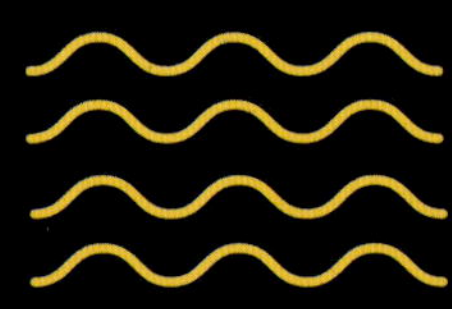

It takes Earth **365.26 days,** or **1 Earth year,** to **ORBIT THE SUN.**

If you're standing at the **EQUATOR,** you're **SPINNING AROUND** Earth's **AXIS** at **1,670** KPH (1,038mph).

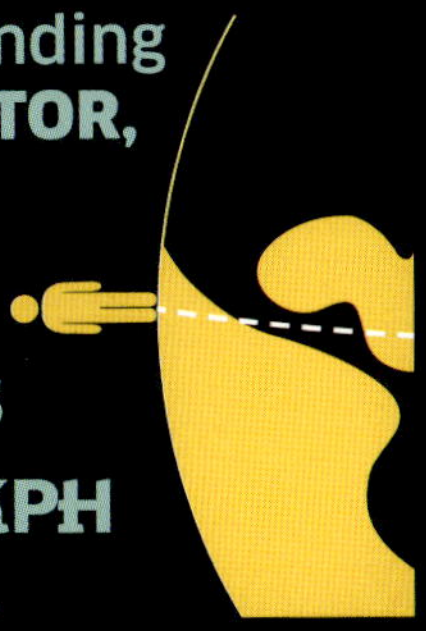

Earth **ORBITS THE SUN** at an **AVERAGE** distance of **149,597,870.7** KM (92,955,807.3 miles). This measure is **1 ASTRONOMICAL UNIT (AU).**

Earth **ROTATES** at an angle of **23.4 degrees** compared to the plane of its orbit. This tilt is the reason for our **SEASONS.**

Objects falling toward Earth will **SPEED UP** at an average of **9.8** m/s (32ft/s) **EVERY SECOND** due to the planet's **GRAVITATIONAL PULL.**

The planet **ORBITS THE SUN** at a **velocity** of **29.8** KM (18.5 miles) per second.

Earth is not perfectly round. It's an **oblate spheroid,** with a **DIAMETER** **42** KM (26 miles) **WIDER AT THE EQUATOR** than at the **POLES.**

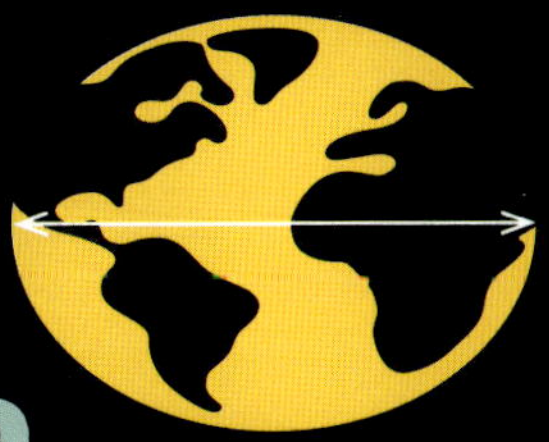

Earth has a **DIAMETER** of **12,760** KM (7,926 miles) at the **EQUATOR.**

With its super-heavy core, Earth is the **DENSEST PLANET** in the Solar System and has a **MASS** of **5.972 SEXTILLION TONNES.** (That's 5,972 with 18 zeroes after it.)

Earth **LOSES** about **50,000** **TONNES** of mass every year, mostly from the **ATMOSPHERE.**

SOLAR SYSTEM

Earth is one of eight planets orbiting the Sun, our nearest star. Together with hundreds of moons, millions of asteroids, countless comets, and space dust, they make up the Solar System. It is just one solar system of thousands we know of in the Milky Way, a 13.6-billion-year-old spiral galaxy.

THE SUN makes up **98%** of the Solar System's **MASS.**

More than **40 space missions** have been sent from **EARTH** to **MARS** over the last **60 years.**

Mostly made of fragments of **WATER ICE,** **SATURN'S RINGS** are just **10 m** (33ft) thick in places.

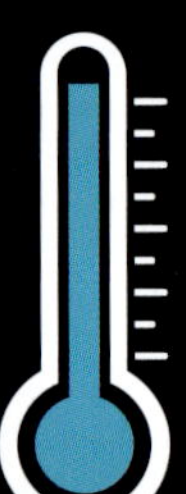

The **HOTTEST PLANET** in the Solar System is **Venus. CARBON DIOXIDE** in its atmosphere traps in heat, sending temperatures soaring to **470°C** (880°F).

The **HIGHEST MOUNTAIN** in the Solar System is **OLYMPUS MONS,** a **VOLCANO** on **MARS** rising **26 KM** (16 miles) high, almost **3 times** the height of **QOMOLANGMA FENG** (Mount Everest).

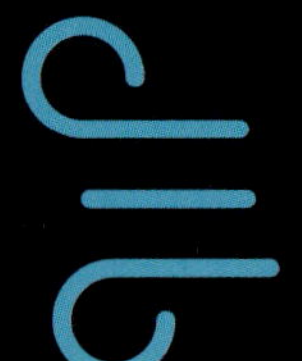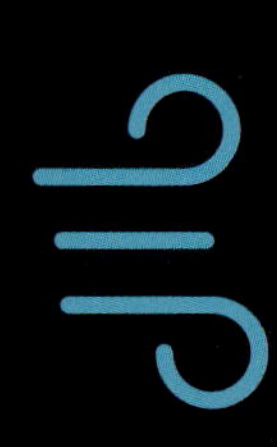

NEPTUNE has the **FASTEST WINDS** in the Solar System. They can reach speeds of **1,200 KPH** (700mph), **9 times** stronger than Earth's.

JUPITER'S MOON GANYMEDE is the **LARGEST** in the Solar System. With a diameter of **5,268 KM** (3,272 miles), it is larger than the planet **MERCURY.**

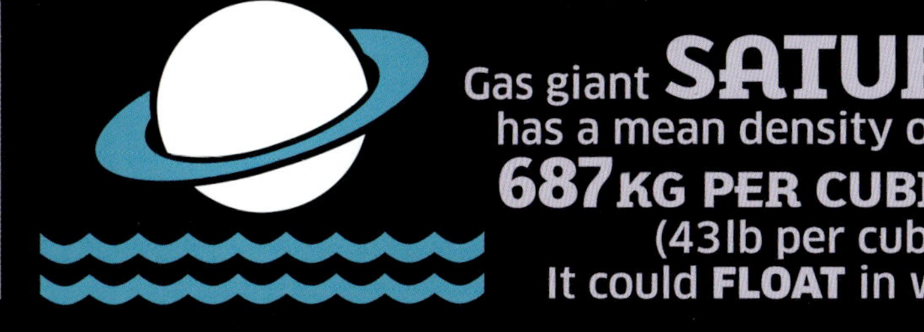

Gas giant **SATURN** has a mean density of just **687 KG PER CUBIC M** (43lb per cubic ft). It could **FLOAT** in water.

The **GREAT RED SPOT** on **JUPITER** is a **STORM** about **16,350 KM** (10,159 miles) wide, estimated to have been spinning for over **300 years.**

Light from the **SUN** takes **8 MINUTES** and **20 SECONDS** to reach Earth.

NEPTUNE has the **LONGEST YEAR** of all the planets. It takes **165 Earth years** to orbit the Sun.

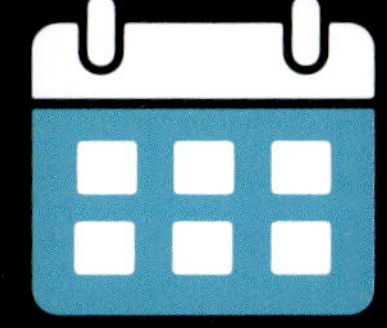

SATURN has the **MOST MOONS, 146** by current estimates.

EARTH HISTORY

Earth began as a super-hot ball of molten rock, regularly hit by rocks from space. Over millions of years, gases were released from the young planet's rocks and volcanoes, creating an atmosphere. Water vapour condensed to form oceans, and supercontinents broke up and formed new land masses.

EARTH'S HISTORY is divided into **4 eons:** the **HADEAN, ARCHEAN, PROTEROZOIC,** and **PHANEROZOIC.**

About **100 million** years after Earth formed, it may have been **HIT** by a **SMALLER PLANET** resulting in the formation of the **MOON.**

During the Hadean (up to 4 billion years ago), **OCEAN TEMPERATURES** reached **230°C** (446°F) – far above boiling point. This was due to **HIGH ATMOSPHERIC PRESSURE.**

The oldest Earth rocks date back to the **HADEAN,** more than **4 BILLION YEARS AGO.**

RODINIA, the **FIRST-KNOWN SUPERCONTINENT,** broke apart some **750 million** years ago.

Earth's first **CONTINENTS** began to form about **4 billion** years ago, from masses of **VOLCANIC ISLANDS.**

For the first **600,000,000 years** of Earth's history, there was **NO LIFE** on the planet.

EARTH DAYS may have been just **6 hours** long when the planet first formed.

Earth formed from a **DISC OF GAS AND DUST** orbiting around the early Sun. The dust eventually clumped together to make rocky **PLANETESIMALS, TENS TO SEVERAL HUNDRED KILOMETRES** across, which then clumped together to make Earth.

Earth gained its **MAGNETIC FIELD** about **3.5 billion** years ago.

Oceans in the **ARCHEAN EON** (4 to 2.5 billion years ago) were **1.5** to **2 TIMES SALTIER** than today.

The **SUN** was **25%** less bright during the Archean than it is now.

If **ALL EARTH HISTORY** was condensed into **a day,** humans would not appear until **11:58**PM.

About **2.7 billion** years ago, bacteria began producing **OXYGEN** through **PHOTOSYNTHESIS,** as plants do today.

Around **2.33 BILLION** years ago, there was a **SUDDEN INCREASE** in the amount of **OXYGEN** in Earth's atmosphere, which killed off **80%** of the **SIMPLE LIFE** that had evolved.

The Moon is

384,400km (238,855 miles) away

from **EARTH** on average – that's further than travelling 9½ times round **THE EQUATOR.**

The Moon is around *80 times* **LIGHTER** than Earth.

In **2024**, scientists located a **CAVE** on the Moon for the **FIRST** time. At around

100m

(328ft) deep, it could be used as a **lunar base** for humans.

The bottom of some **MOON CRATERS** can be as cold as **−173°C** (−279.4°F). Earth's lowest recorded temperature was **−89.2°C** (−128.6°F) in Vostok, Antarctica.

In direct sunshine, the **TEMPERATURE** on the Moon can reach

127°C

(260.6°F). Water boils at **100°C** (212°F)!

Most scientists think our Moon formed when a Mars-sized planet crashed into Earth. Debris from the collision clustered together to create the Moon. Earth's companion is the fifth-largest moon in our Solar System. It appears to glow in the night sky because light from the Sun reflects off its surface.

At **27%** the size of Earth, our Moon is the **LARGEST MOON** in the Solar System relative to the size of its planet.

Tests on **ROCK SAMPLES** brought back by the **Apollo 17** mission prove that the Moon is at least **4.46 billion** years old.

Between **1969** and **1972**, **12 ASTRONAUTS** walked on the **MOON'S SURFACE.**

The Moon's **surface gravity** is about ⅙ of Earth's, so you could jump **6 TIMES** higher there!

The Moon is **MOVING AWAY** from Earth – but only by **38mm** (1½in) **EACH YEAR.**

The Moon takes **27.3 days** to **ORBIT** around Earth.

One lunar month, which is equivalent to **29.5 Earth days,** is how long it takes the **PHASES OF THE MOON** to repeat.

The Moon has **MOONQUAKES.** With the strongest reaching **5.7** on the Richter scale, they are weaker than earthquakes but can last **HOURS** instead of seconds.

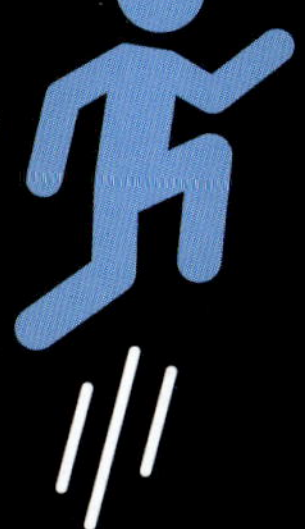

Only around **60%** of the **MOON'S SURFACE** can be seen from Earth.

Super SPACE ROCKS

Asteroids and meteoroids are rocky objects in space that are much smaller than planets. Asteroids are over 1m (3ft) in diameter, meteoroids less than this. When meteoroids enter Earth's atmosphere, they may burn up as meteors, or shooting stars. If space rocks hit the ground, they are called meteorites.

To date, **1,417,544 asteroids** and **dwarf planets** have been observed in the Solar System.

An asteroid **150m** (450ft) wide hits Earth about every **10,000** years.

An estimated **44 tonnes** of **METEORITIC MATERIAL** falls towards Earth **EACH DAY.**

More than **50,000 meteorites** have been found on Earth. **99.8%** of these are fragments of **asteroids.**

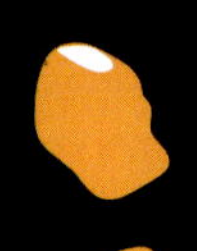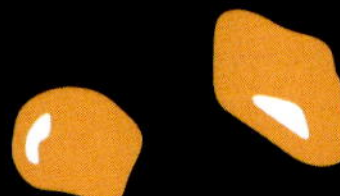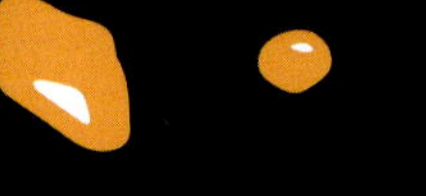

The **ASTEROID BELT** between **MARS** and **JUPITER** forms a ring that stretches **315** to **480 MILLION KM** (195 to 300 million miles) from the Sun.

METEOR SHOWERS are caused when the Earth passes through the dust trail of a **comet,** resulting in up to **100 SHOOTING STARS** per **HOUR.**

In 2013, a **house-sized meteorite** raced across the sky above **CHELYABINSK, RUSSIA,** at **18 KM** (11 miles) **PER SECOND** before breaking apart.

Most **SHOOTING STARS** are caused by meteoroids the size of a **GRAIN OF SAND** burning about **100 KM** (62 miles) above Earth.

The **1.2 km-** (3,900ft-) wide
BARRINGER CRATER
in **ARIZONA, USA**, is the result of a
METEORITE 50 m (165ft) across
hitting Earth about **50,000** years ago.

The **ASTEROID BELT** is mostly empty
space with objects an average
965,600 km
(600,000 miles) apart.

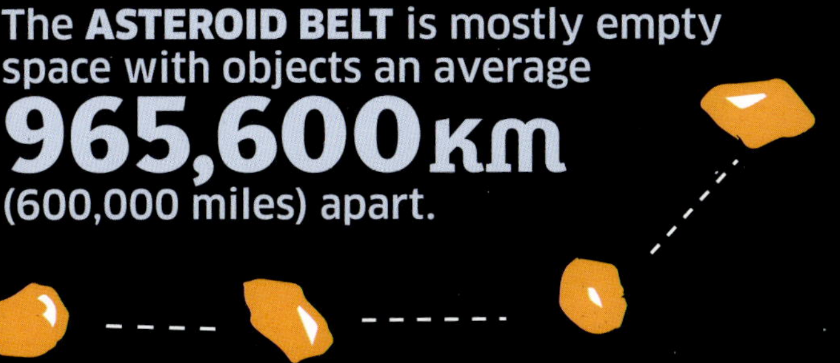

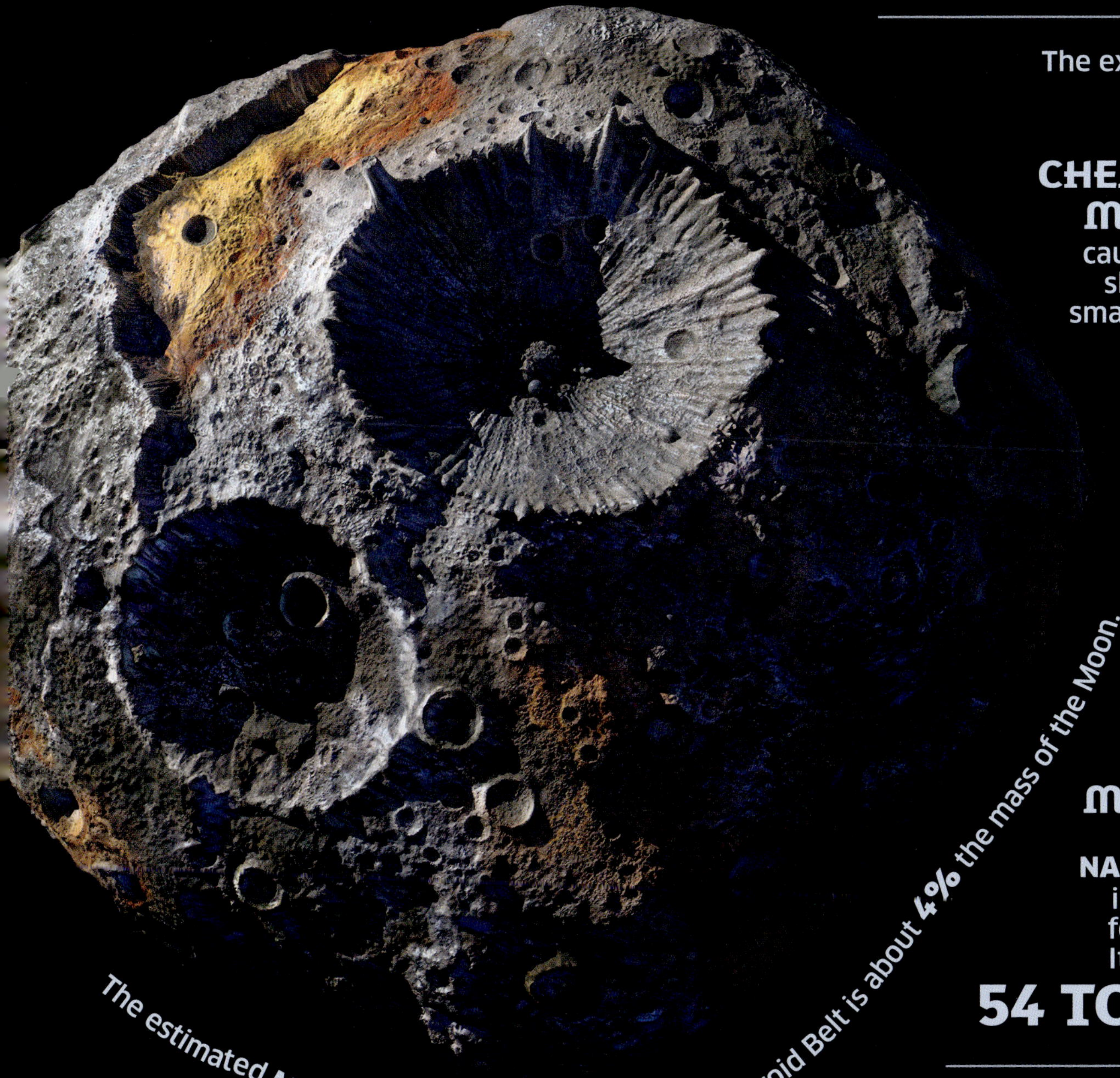

The explosion of the
2013
CHELYABINSK METEORITE
caused a massive
shockwave that
smashed windows
in more than
3,600
apartment
blocks.

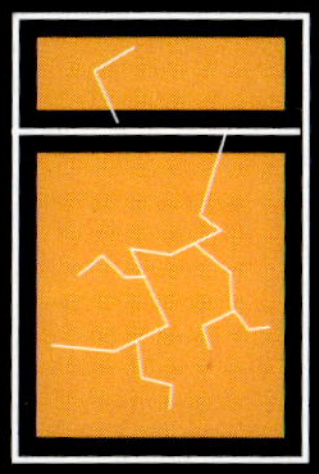

The **HOBA METEORITE** discovered in
NAMIBIA in **1920**
is the **LARGEST**
found on Earth.
It weighs about
54 TONNES.

The estimated **MASS** of all the space rocks in the Asteroid Belt is about **4%** the mass of the Moon.

The **Asteroid Belt** is thought
to be the **LEFTOVER ROCKS** from the
formation of the **SOLAR SYSTEM**
4.55 billion years ago.

The **LARGEST OBJECT**
in the Asteroid Belt
is the dwarf planet
CERES.
It measures
952 km
(592 miles) in diameter.

AUROROS

This colourful phenomenon, also known as the Northern or Southern Lights, is caused by storms on the Sun's surface. These produce energized particles carried in solar winds that slam into Earth's atmosphere. Some interact with our planet's magnetic field and speed towards the North and South Poles, creating fantastic displays in the night sky.

THE NORTHERN LIGHTS are most visible close to the **Arctic Circle,** which is **66.5° NORTH** of the **Equator.**

The fastest **solar winds** that travel through space from the Sun can reach **SPEEDS** of around **800 KM** (497 miles) **A SECOND.**

The **SUN'S ACTIVITY** roughly repeats itself on an **11-year CYCLE,** which affects the **BRIGHTNESS** of the **auroras** seen on Earth.

GREEN AURORAS appear at roughly **100—250 KM** (60–150 miles) above the surface of Earth, and **RED AURORAS** occur roughly **200 KM** (125 miles) and higher.

The Northern Lights, which are also called the **AURORA BOREALIS,** occur **24 HOURS A DAY.** However, it's easiest to see them at **NIGHT** between **LATE SEPTEMBER** and **EARLY APRIL,** when the sky is darkest.

The particles in the **solar wind** take between **2** and **5 DAYS** to reach Earth.

Auroras that occur around the **SOUTH POLE** are known as the **SOUTHERN LIGHTS**. Their Latin name, *Aurora Australis*, was coined by **CAPTAIN JAMES COOK**, who first saw them on a **1770** **VOYAGE TO AUSTRALIA.**

ASTRONAUTS on the **INTERNATIONAL SPACE STATION, 400 KM** (249 miles) above Earth, often **LOOK DOWN** on the Northern Lights.

Recordings made in **FINLAND** suggest that around **5%** of the strongest auroras make noises, such as **crackling** and **hissing.**

It's thought the **NORTHERN LIGHTS** appear in prehistoric **Cro-Magnon CAVE PAINTINGS,** which are more than **30,000 YEARS OLD.**

MUCH BRIGHTER auroras than the Northern Lights occur on **Jupiter** because that planet's **magnetic field** is **20,000 TIMES STRONGER** than Earth's.

The **2 main gases** in Earth's atmosphere are **NITROGEN,** which creates **PURPLE** and **BLUE** auroras, and **OXYGEN,** which produces **GREEN** and **RED** auroras.

The **FIRST-KNOWN SCIENTIFIC ACCOUNT** of the Northern Lights was written around **2,350 YEARS AGO** – by **Aristotle** in the **4TH CENTURY BCE.**

During the **CAMBRIAN EXPLOSION,** which took place **541 MILLION** to **530 MILLION YEARS** ago, **20** of the **35 MAJOR ANIMAL GROUPS** started to appear.

More than **65,000 CAMBRIAN-PERIOD** fossils have been found in **CANADA'S BURGESS SHALE SITE,** including **19** types of **trilobite.**

Scientists believe the **FIRST PLANTS ON LAND** appeared more than **500 MILLION** years ago and were **mosses** and **liverworts.**

An animal with a **BACKBONE** inside its body, like humans, is called a **VERTEBRATE.** The earliest were **JAWLESS FISH** that lived around **520 MILLION** years ago.

EARLY LIFE

Simple, single-celled organisms appeared in our seas billions of years ago during the Precambrian Period. However, the earliest life on Earth did not leave much of a trace in the fossil record. It wasn't until the Cambrian explosion, which began around 540 million years ago, that many new animals started emerging in an enormous variety of forms.

Nearly **90%** of **EARTH'S HISTORY** happened before the **CAMBRIAN EXPLOSION.**

EARTH had existed **600 MILLION YEARS** before life appeared on the planet.

The **FIRST LIFE FORMS** were probably **TINY MICROBES.** Traces of them have been **FOUND IN ROCKS** that are **3.7 BILLION YEARS OLD.**

21% of our **AIR** is **OXYGEN,** which humans need to survive. However, **2.3 BILLION YEARS** ago, the air only contained about **1% OXYGEN.**

Sponges were among the **FIRST ANIMALS** to evolve. The **OLDEST-KNOWN ANIMAL FOSSIL** is a **1.2 mm** (0.05 in) **SPONGE,** the size of a grain of rice.

Dickinsonia looked like a **FLAT, OVAL WORM** and ranged in size from less than **4 mm** (⅙ in) long to almost **1 m** (39 in).

The **20 cm-** (8 in-) tall *Auroralumina attenboroughii* is the **EARLIEST-KNOWN ANIMAL PREDATOR.** It captured food in its **TENTACLES.**

The **EARLIEST-KNOWN** animal with **HARD BODY PARTS,** *Coronacollina acula*, dates to **560 MILLION YEARS AGO.** It had at least **4 spikes** supporting its **THIMBLE-LIKE BODY.**

There were

3 extinctions

during the **DEVONIAN PERIOD**, about **10 MILLION YEARS APART** and ending around **360 MILLION YEARS AGO**. Since mainly tropical animals died out, the extinctions were probably due to **GLOBAL COOLING**.

NON-AVIAN DINOSAURS were wiped out by an **ASTEROID** about **12 KM** (7.5 miles) across hitting waters off Mexico's **YUCATÁN PENINSULA 66 MILLION YEARS AGO.**

More than

45,300

SPECIES are currently **THREATENED** with **EXTINCTION**, including **41% of AMPHIBIANS, 26% of MAMMALS,** and **12% OF BIRDS.**

The **END-TRIASSIC EXTINCTION** around **201 million YEARS AGO** corresponded with the **BREAKUP** of the supercontinent **PANGAEA** and paved the way for dinosaurs to dominate.

99%

More than of all **PLANTS** and **ANIMALS** that have ever lived on Earth are **EXTINCT**.

The last *Homo neanderthalensis,* our **CLOSEST ANCIENT HUMAN RELATIVE**, died about **39,000 YEARS AGO.**

It took about **10 MILLION YEARS** for the planet to **RECOVER** from the **GREAT DYING**.

EXTINCTION RATES are now between **100** and **1,000 TIMES HIGHER** than the rate through **NATURAL EVOLUTION.**

A **sixth MASS EXTINCTION** is possible due to **human activity,** such as **FARMING, OVER-HARVESTING OF SPECIES,** and **GREENHOUSE GAS EMISSIONS.**

The **COELACANTH** is a species of **FISH** that was thought to have died out

66 MILLION

years ago with the dinosaurs until it was rediscovered in **1938.**

EXTINCTIONS

In Earth's history there have been five major extinction events. Each of them wiped out over 75 per cent of all living species. Extinctions have been caused by climate change, volcanic activity, changes in the chemistry of the oceans, and asteroid impacts.

The asteroid that killed the dinosaurs hit Earth at **90,000 KPH (56,000mph).**

The **WORST EXTINCTION** in Earth's history took place **252 MILLION YEARS AGO.** In the **"Great Dying"**, as much as **96%** of all marine species and about **75%** of land species died out.

During the Great Dying, sea surface temperatures at the **EQUATOR** were **40°C** (104°F), as **hot as a bath.** No fish could survive this.

One cause of the **GREAT DYING** was major **VOLCANIC ERUPTIONS** in what is now **SIBERIA,** with **3 MILLION CUBIC KM** (720,000 cubic miles) of **LAVA** released.

444 MILLION years ago, before the first land animals, the Earth **COOLED DRAMATICALLY** and **SEA LEVELS DROPPED,** leading to **85%** of **marine species** dying out.

ROCKY PLANET

EARTH'S STRUCTURE

Earth has three primary layers: a thin outer crust, a deep solid rock mantle, and a core made mostly of iron and nickel under huge pressure. The outer core is molten and the inner core is solid. The crust is made up of tectonic plates that cause earthquakes and volcanoes where they collide or move apart.

84% of Earth's volume is made up of the **MANTLE** that lies beneath the crust. The **CORE** makes up **15%** and the **CRUST** just **1%**.

Earth's mantle is an average of **2,900 KM** (1,800 miles) thick.

CRATONS (gigantic, stable pieces of the crust and upper mantle) are found in every continent and contain rocks that are **2.5–4 billion years old.**

The **DEEPEST HUMAN-MADE HOLE** into Earth's crust is the **KOLA SUPERDEEP BOREHOLE**, a **12.3 KM** (7.6 mile) shaft near **ZAPOLYARNY, RUSSIA.**

The solid **INNER CORE** of **IRON** and **NICKEL** has an average temperature of **5,000°C** (9,900°F), about the same as the **SURFACE OF THE SUN.**

The **PRESSURE** at Earth's inner core is nearly **3.6 million atmospheres** (3,600,000 **TIMES** air pressure at sea level).

Compared to the rest of the planet, the **LIQUID OUTER CORE** makes **one extra rotation** every **1,000 years.**

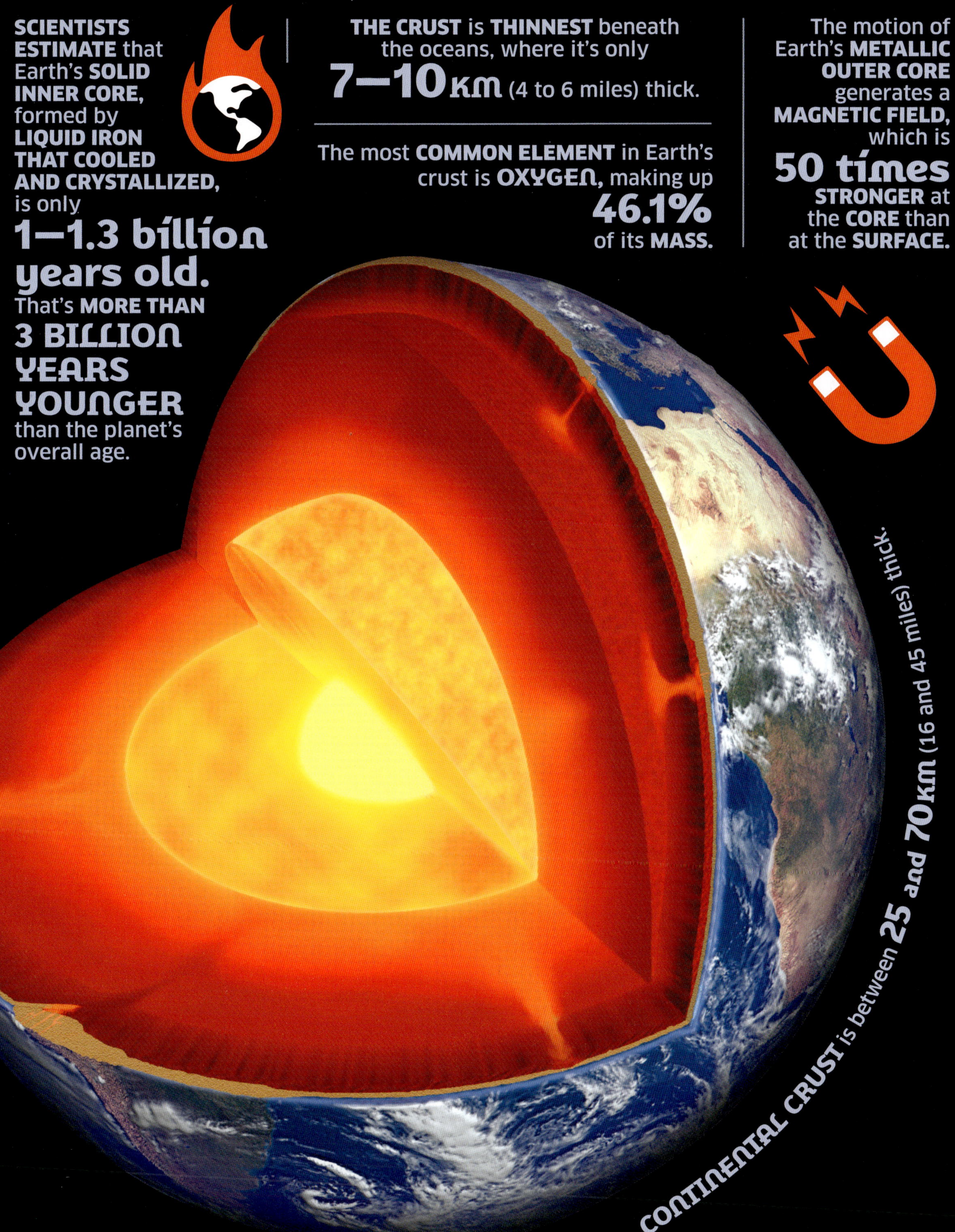

SCIENTISTS ESTIMATE that Earth's SOLID INNER CORE, formed by LIQUID IRON THAT COOLED AND CRYSTALLIZED, is only 1–1.3 billion years old. That's MORE THAN 3 BILLION YEARS YOUNGER than the planet's overall age.

THE CRUST is THINNEST beneath the oceans, where it's only 7–10 KM (4 to 6 miles) thick.

The most COMMON ELEMENT in Earth's crust is OXYGEN, making up 46.1% of its MASS.

The motion of Earth's METALLIC OUTER CORE generates a MAGNETIC FIELD, which is 50 times STRONGER at the CORE than at the SURFACE.

CONTINENTAL CRUST is between 25 and 70 KM (16 and 45 miles) thick.

PLATES AND CONTINENTS

Earth's crust and upper mantle is divided into tectonic plates that move slowly over the planet's mantle. Where they collide, one plate can be pushed up to form a mountain range or down to form a deep trench. Continental plates carry the planet's large land masses, the continents, and gradually shift their positions.

Between **335** and **200 million YEARS AGO**, all of Earth's continents were joined as one **SUPERCONTINENT** called **PANGAEA.**

By most counts, there are **7 continents** on Earth. From largest to smallest they are **ASIA, AFRICA, NORTH AMERICA, SOUTH AMERICA, ANTARCTICA, EUROPE,** and **AUSTRALIA.**

TECTONIC PLATES MOVE between **2.5—15cm** (1–6in) **A YEAR.** The average plate moves as fast as your **fingernails** grow.

Scientists believe the continents of **NORTH AMERICA** and **ASIA** will join and form a new **SUPERCONTINENT, AMASIA,** in **50** to **200 MILLION YEARS.**

THE ANDES mountains started forming when the **NAZCA PLATE** began moving under the **SOUTH AMERICAN PLATE** around **170 MILLION YEARS AGO.**

7 MAJOR TECTONIC PLATES make up around **95%** of Earth's **LAND MASS.** Smaller plates make up the rest.

Even though they're often seen as separate continents, **EUROPE** and **ASIA** occupy only **1 TECTONIC PLATE.**

The **SAN ANDREAS FAULT** on the West Coast of **NORTH AMERICA** is a **1,200km-** (750 mile-) long boundary where **2 plates** are moving **PAST EACH OTHER.**

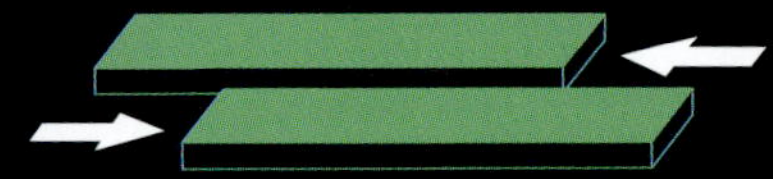

SILFRA RIFT is a **600m** (2,000 ft) fissure opened by an **EARTHQUAKE.**

The **AFRICAN PLATE** started splitting into **2 SEPARATE** continental plates around **25 MILLION YEARS AGO.** The split may create a **sixth ocean.**

The continents of **NORTH** and **SOUTH AMERICA** came together about **3 million years ago.**

At **ICELAND'S Silfra Rift,** you can **SWIM** between **2 PLATES:** the North American and Eurasian.

THE PACIFIC PLATE is an oceanic tectonic plate, and the **LARGEST,** at **103 million SQ KM** (40 million sq miles).

The **YOUNGEST** parts of the **OCEAN FLOOR** are found along the **16,000 KM-** (10,000 mile-) long **Mid–Atlantic Ridge,** which borders **4 PLATES** that are moving apart from each other.

The **AUSTRALIAN PLATE** is drifting **NORTHWARDS** at **7cm** a rate of around (2.8in) a year.

NEW ZEALAND lies on a **MICROCONTINENT,** or possible **EIGHTH CONTINENT,** named **Zealandía,** that's **94%** **UNDERWATER.**

The **LARGEST FRESHWATER LAKE** in the world by surface area is **LAKE SUPERIOR,** on the Canada/USA border, measuring **82,098 SQ KM** (31,698 sq miles).

Canada has **48 NATIONAL PARKS** and reserves. The biggest, **WOOD BUFFALO,** at **44,807 SQ KM** (17,300 sq miles), is larger than **SWITZERLAND.**

The **UNITED STATES** is made up of **50 STATES** including **ALASKA,** which is west of Canada, and the **137 ISLANDS** of **HAWAII.**

The **Panama Canal** is a **82 KM-** (50 mile-) long **WATERWAY CUT THROUGH** the narrow strip of land joining **NORTH AND SOUTH AMERICA.**

At its **CLOSEST** point, **ALASKA** is just **85 KM** (53 miles) across the **BERING STRAIT** from Russia.

There are about **91.9 million CATTLE** on **US FARMS, 1 COW** for every **3.6 PEOPLE.**

The **LONGEST RIVER** in North America is the **MISSOURI,** which winds **3,768 KM** (2,341 miles) from **MONTANA** to **MISSOURI,** USA, where it joins the **MISSISSIPPI.**

THE BAHAMAS in the Caribbean is made up of about **700 ISLANDS,** but **69.9%** of the population live on **JUST ONE ISLAND –** New Providence.

NORTH AMERICA

North America is the third-largest continent in the world. It stretches from the icy Aleutian Islands in the northwest to the Isthmus of Panama in the south, where it joins South America. The continent includes Canada, the United States of America, Mexico, Greenland, and the Caribbean Islands.

The **WETTEST** place in North America is **HUCUKTLIS LAKE** (Henderson Lake) on **VANCOUVER ISLAND, CANADA,** which receives an average **7 m** (23ft) of **RAIN A YEAR.**

The **HIGHEST POINT** in North America is the top of **DENALI** (Mount McKinley) in Alaska, USA, at **6,190 m** (20,310ft).

The **HIGHEST RECORDED AIR TEMPERATURE** on Earth was **57°C** (134˚F), measured at **DEATH VALLEY, CALIFORNIA, USA, in 1913.**

The largest city in **NORTH AMERICA** is **MEXICO CITY,** with a population of about **9 million.**

The **ICE SHEET** over **GREENLAND** is **3 KM** (1.9 miles) **DEEP** in places.

Including all of its islands, **CANADA** has the **LONGEST COASTINE** of any country in the world – **202,080 KM** (125,567 miles).

About **90%** of people in **CANADA** live **WITHIN 160 KM** (100 miles) of the **BORDER** with the **USA.**

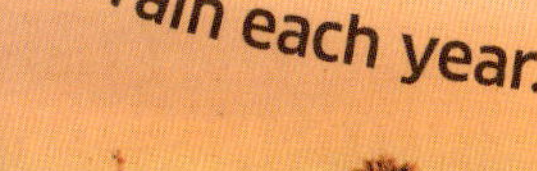

SOUTH AMERICA was the stomping ground for what may be the **LARGEST-KNOWN LAND CREATURE –** a **DINOSAUR** called *ARGENTINOSAURUS HUINCULENSIS*, which weighed at least

60 TONNES.

A plant known as the

Queen of the Andes,
PUYA RAIMONDII, is one of the **LARGEST HERBS** in the world and can be

9m
(29ft 6in) **TALL.**

SOUTH AMERICA covers about

17,814,000

SQ KM (6,878,025 sq miles) – roughly **1/8** of Earth's **TOTAL** land surface.

The **ANDES**, the longest mountain range on land, spans **7 SOUTH AMERICAN COUNTRIES.**

ARGENTINA contains **MOUNT ACONCAGUA,** South America's **HIGHEST POINT** at

6,962m

(22,840ft) above sea level, and its **LOWEST POINT, LAGUNA DEL CARBÓN** at

105m

(345ft) below sea level.

The **ATACAMA DESERT** in Chile is the **driest region in the world** outside Antarctica, with around

1mm

(0.04in) of rainfall each year.

SOUTH AMERICA

This continent lies mostly in the Southern Hemisphere. It contains the dense Amazon rainforest, vast fertile grasslands called the Pampas, the often snow-capped Andes mountains, and the driest non-polar desert in the world, the Atacama.

Comparing its **LENGTH** to its **WIDTH**, Earth's longest and narrowest country is **CHILE**. It is **4,300 KM** (2,672 miles) long and has an average width of **175 KM** (109 miles).

The **Pampas** are a stretch of **GRASSY PLAINS** that cover **1.2 million SQ KM** (463,000 sq miles) of South America.

The **WORLD'S WIDEST RIVER**, the **AMAZON**, empties **209,000 cubic metres** (7,380,765 cubic ft) of fresh water – enough to fill **69 OLYMPIC SWIMMING POOLS** – into the **ATLANTIC OCEAN EVERY SECOND.**

There are over **3,550 BIRD SPECIES** in **SOUTH AMERICA** – more than in any other continent.

There are around **100 TRIBES** in the world that have **NO CONTACT** with other humans – **more than ½** live in the **AMAZON RAINFOREST.**

South America's **MOST POPULATED** city is **São Paulo** in Brazil. Around **20.4 million** people live there.

The flat-topped **MOUNT RORAIMA** is **14 KM** (9 miles) long and found where the borders of **3 countries** (Venezuela, Guyana, and Brazil) meet.

19% of Europe's **PLANT** and **ANIMAL SPECIES** are currently at risk of *extinction.*

With around **13 MILLION** people, **MOSCOW, RUSSIA,** has the **BIGGEST POPULATION** of any European city.

Hum, CROATIA, is purportedly the world's **SMALLEST** town. The **MEDIEVAL SETTLEMENT** atop a hill has a population of **under 30.**

At least **7 VILLAGES** in **NORWAY** are known by just **1 LETTER — Å.**

There are **14 COUNTRIES** in Europe with **GLACIERS.** The **SOUTHERNMOST** is in **BULGARIA.**

Europe has **44 countries,** **27 OF WHICH** are members of the **EUROPEAN UNION.**

More than **200** different languages are spoken in Europe, but only **24 OF THESE** are listed as **OFFICIAL LANGUAGES** by the **EUROPEAN UNION.**

VALLETTA, MALTA, is the **HOTTEST** place in Europe, with an average daily high of **22.3°C** (72.1°F).

At **3,469 m** (11,380ft) above sea level, the **PICO DE VELETA** in Spain is Europe's **HIGHEST PAVED MOUNTAIN ROAD.**

Europe's largest active volcano, **MOUNT ETNA** in Sicily, is **3,329 m** (10,920ft) tall and has **ERUPTED** around **200 TIMES** in the last **3,500 years.**

Trees cover **40%** of Europe, making it one of the most **FORESTED** places on Earth.

EUROPE

Found mostly on the Eurasian Plate it shares with Asia, Europe is the second-smallest continent, but it has lots of people – more than either North or South America. Most areas of Europe have four seasons with warm summers and cold winters, but some of its Mediterranean climes can be hot and sunny all year round.

At **0.49 SQ KM** (0.189 sq miles), **VATICAN CITY** is not just the **SMALLEST** country in **EUROPE** – it's the **SMALLEST** in the **WORLD**.

SAN MARINO is the world's **OLDEST** existing **REPUBLIC**. It was founded in the **YEAR 301** and now has a population of around **29,000**.

Norway is Europe's **EIGHTH-LARGEST** country, but has the continent's **LONGEST COASTLINE** at **101,390 KM** (63,000 miles) – only **CANADA'S** is longer.

MONT BLANC is the **TALLEST** peak in the Alps, at more than **4,800 m** (15,760ft).

A **NEOLITHIC MAN, MUMMIFIED** around **5,300 years ago,** was found in a **GLACIER** in **ITALY'S TYROLEAN ALPS**. His is the world's **OLDEST HUMAN BODY PRESERVED IN ICE.**

The **Alps** are formed of **3 MOUNTAIN RANGES** arcing across **8 EUROPEAN COUNTRIES**.

AFRICA

The second-largest continent on Earth, Africa is a land of desert, savanna, and rainforest. It is the hottest continent, most of it lies between the Tropics of Cancer and Capricorn. Africa is also the birthplace of humanity, where the first *Homo sapiens* appeared over 315,000 years ago.

AFRICA AND ALL ITS ISLANDS make up **20%** of Earth's land surface area – about **30,365,000 SQ KM** (11,724,000 sq miles).

Africa contains the **LONGEST RIVER** in the world. The **NILE** flows for **6,695 KM** (4,160 miles) from **TANZANIA** to **EGYPT**.

There are thought to be **2,000 LANGUAGES** spoken in Africa with **520** spoken in **Nigeria** alone.

Over **1,519,000,000** people – **18.3%** of the world's population – live in Africa.

The **AFRICAN ELEPHANT**, found in **23** countries, is the **LARGEST LIVING LAND ANIMAL** at **7 TONNES**.

Dating to **2.023 billion** years ago, South Africa's **VREDEFORT DOME** is Earth's **OLDEST** and **BIGGEST IMPACT CRATER**.

The highest temperature recorded in Africa was

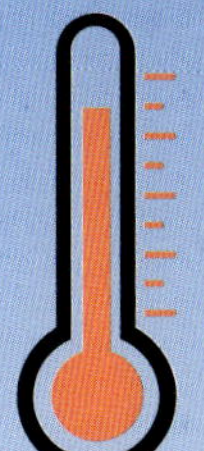

55°C
(131°F) measured in **KEBILI, TUNISIA,** in **1931.**

The **BIGGEST HOT DESERT** in the world, Africa's **SAHARA,** is getting larger. It is now

10%
BIGGER than it was **100** years ago.

The **TALLEST MOUNTAIN** in Africa is **KILIMANJARO** in **TANZANIA,** reaching

5,895m
(19,341ft) above sea level.

Africa has the most countries of any continent –

54.
The **LARGEST** country is **Algeria.**

60% of
Africa is made up of **drylands** and **desert.**

Africa's **MOST POPULOUS** country is **NIGERIA,** with about

230 million
PEOPLE – over **15%** of the continent's population.

The **CONGO BASIN** contains about

3.14
MILLION SQ KM (1.2 million sq miles) of **rainforest.**

The **GREAT RIFT VALLEY** system stretches for about

4,000km
(2,500 miles) through

12
African countries, from **ERITREA** to **MOZAMBIQUE.**

The **MAIN SOURCE** for the River Nile is Africa's **LARGEST LAKE, VICTORIA.** It covers **69,484 SQ KM** (26,828 sq miles).

The **NGORONGORO CRATER** in **TANZANIA** is the result of a **VOLCANO COLLAPSE 2.5 MILLION** years ago. It is home to over **25,000** animals.

ASIA

Asia is the largest of the world's seven continents. Joining Europe in the east, and crossing 11 time zones, Asia contains the world's highest and lowest points, the world's largest and deepest lakes, and the most populous countries.

The most **POPULOUS** country on Earth is **India** with over **1.4 billion** inhabitants – about **17.8%** of the **WORLD'S TOTAL.**

About **60%** of the **WORLD'S POPULATION** lives in **ASIA.**

The **LONGEST RIVER** in Asia is the **CHANG JIANG** (Yangtze River) in **CHINA,** at **6,300 KM** (3,915 miles) in length.

Asia covers about **30%** of **EARTH'S LAND SURFACE.**

The **BIGGEST COUNTRY** in Asia (and the world), Russia, is **57,377 TIMES LARGER** than its **SMALLEST COUNTRY,** the Maldives, a series of **26 coral atolls** with **298 SQ KM** (115 sq miles) of land.

Earth's **LARGEST** human-made structure, the Great Wall of China took **2,000 YEARS** to build.

Indonesia is the **WORLD'S LARGEST ISLAND NATION**, with

13,558 ISLANDS

stretching over **4.57 MILLION SQ KM** (1.76 million sq miles).

THE URAL MOUNTAINS, in **RUSSIA** and **KAZAKHSTAN,** are some of the world's oldest – between **250 and 300 million YEARS OLD.**

INDIA receives about

80%

of its annual rainfall during the summer **monsoon season.**

The **Dead Sea** is a **LAKE** with its surface

430.5m

(1,412ft) **BELOW SEA LEVEL** – the **LOWEST** place on Earth. It is

9.6 times

SALTIER than the ocean.

The **LOWEST TEMPERATURE** outside Antarctica was recorded at **OYMYAKON** in **RUSSIA** in **1933** – a chilling

–67.7°C

(-90°F).

The **Himalaya mountain range** extends for about **2,500km** (1,550 miles) along the **NORTHERN EDGE** of the **INDIAN SUBCONTINENT.**

THE WORLD'S LARGEST CITY by population is **TOKYO, JAPAN,** with around **37.2 million PEOPLE** – that's almost the entire population of Canada!

The **ARABIAN PENINSULA** is the **largest peninsula** in the world at **3.25 MILLION SQ KM** (1.25 million sq miles).

AUSTRALIA

This land mass located between the Pacific and Indian Oceans is Earth's smallest continent but one of its biggest countries. The only continent besides Antarctica that is entirely in the Southern Hemisphere, Australia is mostly arid, with patches of grasslands and rainforest, along with some epic beaches.

Found **15** to **150 KM** (10–90 miles) off the coast of Australia, the **GREAT BARRIER REEF** is the **LARGEST LIVING STRUCTURE** on Earth. Its coral reef system stretches over **348,000 SQ KM** (133,000 sq miles), an area roughly the size of Japan.

The world's **LARGEST MONOLITH ROCK** is **Uluru** in Australia. At **348m** (1,142ft) above the surrounding plain, it's **TALLER** than New York's famous **CHRYSLER BUILDING.**

Australia's **TALLEST MOUNTAIN** is **MOUNT KOSCIUSZKO,** which rises **2,228m** (7,300ft) above sea level.

It is believed that **Uluru** extends at least **2.5 KM** (1.5 miles) **UNDERGROUND.**

Australia has a **LAND AREA** of around **7.69 MILLION SQ KM** (3 million sq miles), but it is still the **SMALLEST CONTINENT.**

Australia is also the world's **sixth- LARGEST COUNTRY** – more than **TWICE AS BIG AS INDIA.**

There are more than **10,000 NAMED BEACHES** in **AUSTRALIA** with **12,175 KM** (7,565 miles) of **SAND DUNES.**

Australia has **8,222** associated **ISLANDS.**

Australia is home to over **27 million people — 80%** of them live **WITHIN 50KM** (30 miles) of the **COAST.**

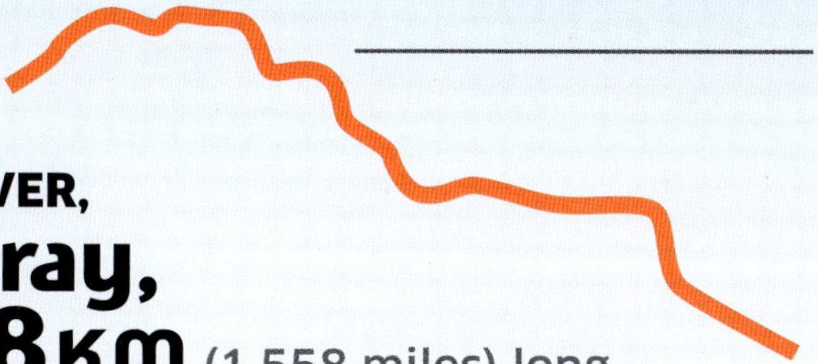

Australia's **LONGEST RIVER,** the **Murray,** is **2,508 KM** (1,558 miles) long, the length of **30 PANAMA CANALS.**

Australia is Earth's **DRIEST INHABITED CONTINENT.** Its land is **18% desert,** with most of the country receiving **LESS THAN 50 cm** (20 in) of **RAIN** per year (½ **THE GLOBAL AVERAGE**).

Most of Australia's plant and animal species are **NOT FOUND ANYWHERE ELSE ON EARTH,** including **87%** of its **MAMMALS** and **93%** of its **REPTILES.**

ANTARCTICA

Antarctica is unlike any other place on Earth. Home to the South Pole, this dry, freezing continent is almost completely covered by ice – the larger East Antarctic Ice Sheet and the thinner West Antarctic Ice Sheet. There are also mountain peaks and snow-free valleys swept by incredibly strong winds.

Icy **ANTARCTICA** is the **third-SMALLEST** continent. Bigger than Europe, it's about **14 million SQ KM** (5.4 million sq miles).

Around **180 million YEARS AGO,** the continent we now call Antarctica was joined to **SOUTH AMERICA, AFRICA,** and **AUSTRALIA** in a land mass called **GONDWANA.**

ANTARCTICA has **zero NATIVE PEOPLE,** but up to **10,000 SCIENTISTS** and around **40,000 TOURISTS** visit each year.

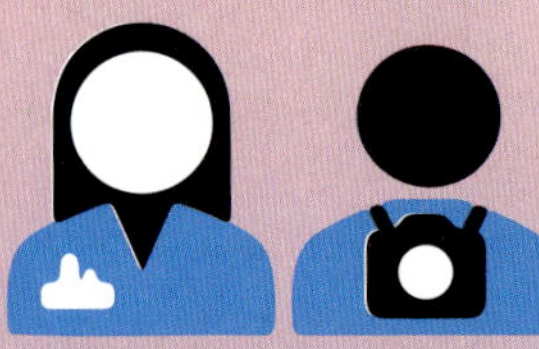

The world's **OLDEST-KNOWN GLACIER ICE** came from Antarctica. It contained **GAS BUBBLES** from at least **2 MILLION years ago.**

ANTARCTICA is the world's **HIGHEST CONTINENT** – the average elevation above sea level is about **2,194 m** (7,200 ft).

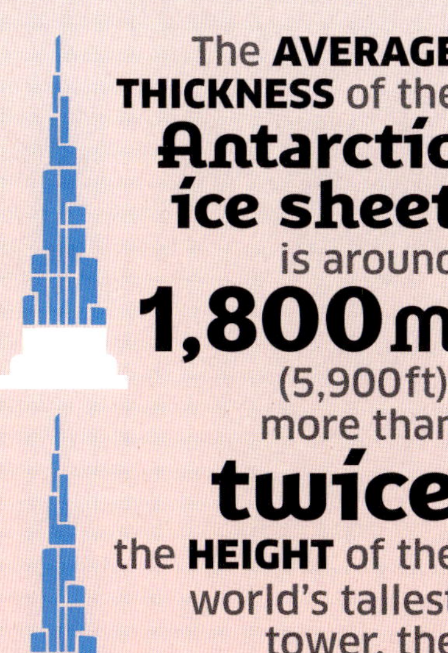

The **AVERAGE THICKNESS** of the **Antarctic ice sheet** is around **1,800 m** (5,900 ft), more than **twice** the **HEIGHT** of the world's tallest tower, the **BURJ KHALIFA.**

THE SOUTH POLE is more than **1,250 km** (777 miles) from the nearest **COASTLINE.**

Antarctica is the **WINDIEST CONTINENT IN THE WORLD –** gusts of more than **325 KPH** (202 mph) have been recorded there.

The **LARGEST-EVER ICEBERG** broke away from the **Ross Ice Shelf** in **2000.** It was a massive **270 KM** (168 miles) long and **40 KM** (25 miles) wide.

ANTARCTICA'S Lake Vostok is the world's **LARGEST UNDERGROUND LAKE.** Almost **4 KM** (2½ miles) below the surface, it contains **2 MILLION** Olympic swimming pools' worth of water.

ANTARCTICA'S DRY VALLEYS cover an area of around **4,000 SQ KM** (1,540 sq miles) and are the world's **COLDEST, DRIEST DESERTS.**

Antarctica's **ICE SHEET** contains about **60%** of the planet's **FRESH WATER.**

MOUNTAIN CHAINS break through the ice. **MOUNT VINSON** is the tallest peak at **4,892 m** (16,050 ft) above sea level.

About **98%** of Antarctica is covered by thick ice. **BRRR!**

Shattering
EARTHQUAKES

Earthquakes are caused by heat from the Earth's core moving tectonic plates in its crust. Waves of seismic energy radiate from a point on the surface called the epicentre. Earthquakes can result in cracks, landslides, tsunamis, and huge damage to buildings and other structures.

About **55** earthquakes happen **every day.** Most are **UNDERWATER** or too **MINOR** to be felt.

Earthquakes are **MEASURED** using the **RICHTER SCALE,** with each number of magnitude **10 times** more powerful than the one below.

The planet experiences an average of **16 MAJOR EARTHQUAKES** (over magnitude 7) **EVERY YEAR.**

23 major earthquakes occurred in **2010,** the **MOST** since records began.

One huge earthquake in **2010** moved the Chilean city of **CONCEPCIÓN 3m** (10ft) further west.

81% of the world's largest earthquakes occur along the **Ring of Fire,** a belt of **VOLCANOES** around the **PACIFIC OCEAN.**

The **deadliest** earthquake recorded happened in **SHAANXI, CHINA,** in 1556 with an estimated **830,000 PEOPLE KILLED.**

CHINA recorded **186 MAJOR EARTHQUAKES** in the past **25 YEARS,** the most of any country.

An **8.9**-magnitude earthquake in **JAPAN** in **2011** shifted Earth's mass, causing it to **SPIN FASTER** and **SHORTENING THE DAY** by **1.8 microseconds.**

The **MOST POWERFUL** earthquake ever recorded took place in **CHILE** on **22 MAY 1960.** It registered as **9.5** on the **RICHTER SCALE.**

Most earthquakes last **10—30 seconds.** The longest-known quake took place near the **SUMATRA-ANDAMAN ISLANDS** and went on for **10 minutes.**

There are **26,000** registered **SEISMOGRAPH STATIONS** worldwide **MONITORING** earthquake activity.

INDONESIA experienced more **EARTHQUAKES** than any other country in **2023**, with over **2,200** above **MAGNITUDE 4.**

EARTHQUAKES can generate **ENORMOUS** ocean waves called **tsunamis.** The **TALLEST** ever recorded reached **524m** (1,720ft). It happened in **1958** after a **7.8-MAGNITUDE EARTHQUAKE** in Alaska, USA, caused a massive **LANDSLIDE** into a bay.

Massive
MOUNTAINS

Mountains are the highest points on Earth. They form in various ways. High mountain ranges can grow where tectonic plates collide, pushing the ground upwards. Other mountains are shaped by erosion or are active or extinct volcanoes, made of cooled molten rock that erupted through Earth's crust.

Officially, a mountain is a **PEAK** with **STEEP SLOPES** that rises **AT LEAST** **300 m** (1,000ft) above its base.

At **8,848.86 m** (29,031ft 8½in), **QOMOLANGMA FENG (MOUNT EVEREST)** is the highest mountain on Earth. It's one of **14 PEAKS** in the **HIMALAYAS** above **8,000M** (26,000ft).

The **OLDEST MOUNTAIN CHAIN** is South Africa's **BARBERTON MAKHONJWA MOUNTAINS**, with rocks dating to **3.6 billion YEARS AGO.**

The **LONGEST MOUNTAIN RANGE** on Earth is

99% underwater.

The Atlantic's **MID-OCEAN RIDGE** spans **65,000 KM** (40,389 miles).

PAKISTAN'S NANGA PARBAT is the **FASTEST-GROWING** mountain, rising **7 mm** (¼ in) every year. It should become Earth's **TALLEST** mountain in **241,000 YEARS.**

OXYGEN LEVELS above **6,000 m** (20,000 ft) in mountains can drop from the normal **21%** to **9.5%** because **AIR** gets **THINNER** higher in the atmosphere.

At **7,570 m** (24,840 ft), **GANGKHAR PUENSUM** in **BHUTAN** is the highest **UNCLIMBED MOUNTAIN,** due to local beliefs that it is **SACRED.**

Measuring from the bottom of the ocean, Earth's **TALLEST PEAK** is **Mauna Kea,** a dormant **VOLCANO** in Hawaii, USA, rising **10,205 m** (33,480 ft) from the seabed.

THE ANDES, ALPS, ROCKIES, AND HIMALAYAS were each formed by the **SLOW COLLISION** of **2 TECTONIC PLATES** over **TENS OF MILLIONS OF YEARS.**

6,664 climbers

have made it to the **SUMMIT** of **QOMOLANGMA FENG** (**MOUNT EVEREST**) since **1953.**

About **24%** of the world's **LAND SURFACE** is covered by mountains.

There are **1,310 PEAKS** over **6,000 m** (20,000 ft) in **NEPAL.**

TOP 10 LONGEST MOUNTAIN RANGES

ANDES MOUNTAINS • South America •
Length: **8,900KM** (5,500 miles)

1

Stretching through seven countries along the entire length of western South America, the Andes are by far the longest continental mountain range on Earth.

2 **GREAT ESCARPMENT** • Africa •
Length: **5,000KM** (3,100 miles)
Jutting up from a strip of coastal land that curves around the southern tip of Africa, this range was formed by rivers eroding the edges of the continent's central plateaus over millions of years.

3 **ROCKIES** • North America • Length: **4,800KM** (3,000 miles)
The USA and Canada's Rocky Mountains are made up of 100 smaller ranges, which are split into four regions spanning Alberta, Canada, to New Mexico, USA.

4 **GREAT DIVIDING RANGE** • Australia •
Length: **3,700KM** (2,300 miles)
Hugging the eastern coast of Australia, the Great Dividing Range is the longest mountain chain found in a single country. Its plateaus and mountains send water down to the Great Artesian Basin.

5 **TRANSANTARCTIC MOUNTAINS** • Antarctica •
Length: **3,200KM** (2,000 miles)
The Transantarctic Mountain range is the world's longest rift shoulder (raised land along on a break in Earth's crust). It stretches from the Weddell Sea to Victoria Land.

6 **APPALACHIAN MOUNTAINS** • North America •
Length: **3,200KM** (2,000 miles)
Some of the oldest mountains on Earth, the rolling Appalachians run from Newfoundland and Labrador in Canada to Alabama in southern USA.

7 **HIMALAYAS** • Asia • Length: **2,600KM** (1,600 miles)
The highest mountain range on Earth, the Himalayas are home to nine of the 10 tallest peaks in the world, including the world's tallest, Qomolangma Feng (Mount Everest).

8 **URAL MOUNTAINS** • Asia and Europe •
Length: **2,500KM** (1,550 miles)
Found mostly in Russia, the Urals stretch from the Kara Sea to the Ural River. They act as the boundary between Asia and Europe, passing through semi-arid and forested landscapes along the way.

9 **TIEN SHAN** • Asia • Length: **2,400KM** (1,490 miles)
This mountain range runs along the border between China and Kyrgyzstan, where its highest point is located – a peak of more than 7,000m (24,000ft).

10 **KUNLUN MOUNTAINS** • Asia • Length: **2,000KM** (1,250 miles)
The Kunluns are in southern Central Asia. The chain rises above a high plateau and is named after the mythical mountain that is a site of paradise in the Taoist tradition.

Cool CAVES

Caves are natural hollows in rock that are large enough for humans to enter. They are usually formed by the weathering of rock when groundwater seeps through cracks. Home to stalactites, stalagmites, and ancient art, caves can have extensive, uncharted networks of underground chambers.

The **SON DOONG CAVE** in **VIETNAM** is the **LARGEST-KNOWN CAVE PASSAGE** in the world, reaching **220 m** (660ft) high and **160 m** (525ft) wide, big enough to house a 40-storey building.

MAMMOTH CAVE in Kentucky, USA, has the world's **LONGEST CAVE SYSTEM** with a combined **LENGTH** of more than **650 KM** (400 miles).

MEXICO'S Cave of Crystals has some of the **LARGEST** crystals ever found – growing up to **4 m** (13ft) **THICK.** It can reach a **SWELTERING 58°C** (136°F) because of the **VOLCANIC VENT** beneath it.

The world's **DEEPEST FRESHWATER CAVE** is about **1,000 m** (3,280ft) deep.

Georgia's **VERËVKINA CAVE** plunges down **2,212 m** (7,257ft), making it the **DEEPEST KNOWN** on Earth.

The world's **OLDEST CAVE ART** depicting a real-life scene is **51,200 YEARS OLD.**

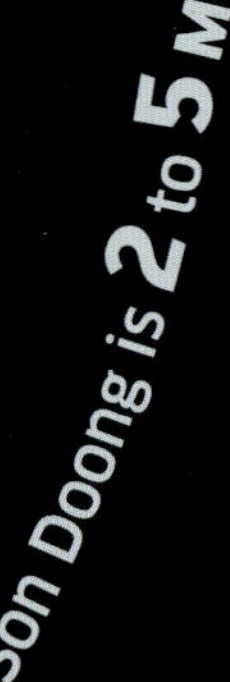

Son Doong is **2 to 5 MILLION YEARS OLD.** Its entrance was discovered in **1991.**

Every summer, a **BAT COLONY** of about

1 million

INHABITS part of **CARLSBAD CAVERN** in New Mexico, USA, known as

Bat Cave.

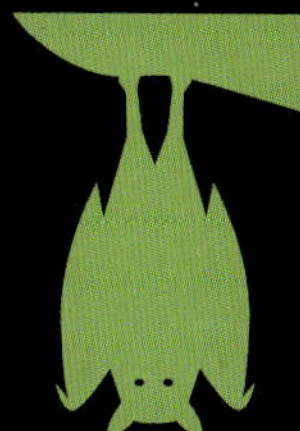

FOSSILS of the oldest-known **HUMAN ANCESTORS**, dating to

3.4

MILLION YEARS AGO, were found in a cave in **SOUTH AFRICA**.

The **OLDEST** layer of ice in Austria's **EISRIESENWELT ICE CAVE** dates back

1,000 years.

Stalactites and **stalagmites** are icicle-like formations caused by **MINERAL-RICH WATER DRIPPING** from cave ceilings. They grow very **SLOWLY**, often just

0.5–2.5cm

(¼–1in) a century.

STALAGMITES grow **UPWARDS** from the cave floor. The **OLDEST-KNOWN** is **2.2 million** years old.

The **RECORD** for the **DEEPEST UNDERWATER**

cave-dive

is **308m** (1,010ft), set in France by **FRÉDÉRIC SWIERCZYNSKI**.

Scotland's **FINGAL'S CAVE** has **6-SIDED** columns of **BASALT** that reach an **ARCHED ROOF**

21m

(72ft) above **SEA LEVEL**.

THE GRAND CANYON

Carved out by the Colorado River over millions of years, the dramatic bends of this canyon display colourful bands of orange and pink sedimentary rock. Arizona's Grand Canyon is one of the widest and deepest river valleys in the world.

The **GRAND CANYON** was named a **NATIONAL PARK** on **26 February 1919.**

6.2 MILLION VISITORS come to the canyon **EACH YEAR.**

The canyon covers **2,678 SQ KM** (1,034 sq miles), an area larger than **THE STATE OF RHODE ISLAND.**

The **GRAND CANYON** runs for **446 KM** (277 miles) along the **COLORADO RIVER** in Arizona, USA.

The canyon is home to around **1,000 CAVES,** but only **335** have been officially documented.

In a **GEOLOGICAL MYSTERY**, there's a **1.2-BILLION-YEAR GAP** between the ages of some side-by-side **ROCK LAYERS** – that's like missing **26%** of **EARTH'S HISTORY.**

The **OLDEST ROCK** in the canyon was formed from **CRYSTALLIZED MAGMA** **1.84 BILLION YEARS AGO.**

EVIDENCE OF HUMAN LIFE in the canyon dates back thousands of years, with **ARTEFACTS** as old as **12,000** YEARS.

The canyon's average depth is **1.6 KM** (1 mile).

There are **5 SPECIES** of **FISH** that are found only in the canyon.

Supaí, the only town in the canyon basin, is **13 KM** (8 miles) from the **NEAREST ROAD** and is the only place where **MULE TRAINS DELIVER THE MAIL.**

Around **6 MILLION YEARS AGO,** the **COLORADO RIVER** began **ERODING** the **ROCKS** into the current canyon formation.

Its **WIDTH** ranges from **200 m** (500ft) to a whopping **29 KM** (18 miles) **ACROSS.**

ZERO DINOSAUR FOSSILS have been found in the **GRAND CANYON.** Its youngest rocks are **20 MILLION YEARS OLDER** than the **EARLIEST DINOSAURS.**

At **YELLOWSTONE PARK**, the water temperature at

200 m

(660ft) deep is

200°C

(392˚F), as hot as an **OVEN**.

The **TALLEST ACTIVE GEYSER** is **STEAMBOAT GEYSER** in Yellowstone National Park, USA. Its tallest spurt shot

137 m

(449ft) high in **2020**.

Geyser eruptions continue

until all the water is forced out or it cools to below water's boiling point,

100°C

(212˚F).

About **½** of Earth's geysers can be found in

Yellowstone National Park,

WYOMING, USA.

The **UNDERGROUND MAGMA CHAMBERS** that heat up **YELLOWSTONE'S GEYSERS** are thought to be between **5** and **48 KM** (3 and 30 miles) below ground.

Not all geysers are **HOT**. Due to a buildup of **CARBON DIOXIDE GAS**, **GEYSIR ANDERNACH** in **GERMANY** fizzes **cold water** through a drilled hole every **90 MINUTES** or so.

An average eruption from Yellowstone's **STEAMBOAT GEYSER** releases

350,000 LITRES

(92,000 gallons) of water, enough to fill about

2,000 BATH TUBS.

STEAMBOAT GEYSER in **YELLOWSTONE** was **INACTIVE** for

50 YEARS

between **1911** and **1961**.

There are estimated to be

1,000 ACTIVE GEYSERS

on Earth.

GEYSERS

Water that seeps through cracks in the Earth's rocks can become superheated. When pressure builds up underground, steam and hot water is forced out through a narrow opening as a jet called a geyser. As the pressure and temperature drop, the water flows back below the surface to heat up again and repeat the cycle.

The **TALLEST** recorded geyser was **WAIMANGU GEYSER,** near Rotorua, **NEW ZEALAND.** Its jets reached over **460 m** (1,500ft) **HIGH** before it became **DORMANT** in 1904.

The most **DEPENDABLE** geyser is **El Jefe** in northern **CHILE,** which **ERUPTS** every **132 SECONDS.**

CUEXCOMATE in **MEXICO** is a **WIDE, INACTIVE GEYSER CONE** that visitors can step **23 m** (75ft) **DOWN INTO.**

El Tatío geysers in **CHILE** are the **HIGHEST** in the world, at an altitude of over **4,300 m** (14,000ft).

The word "GEYSER" comes from **GEYSIR** in **ICELAND,** a **HOT WATER JET** first described over **700 YEARS AGO.**

Boiling
HOT SPRINGS

Hot springs occur when groundwater is naturally heated up by molten or hot rocks. Their waters are always hotter than the surrounding air temperature and rich with dissolved minerals. Some are nice to take a dip in while others are too scalding to touch.

WATER starts to **BURN SKIN** at a temperature of **49°C** (120°F). Hot springs can be **twice** as **HOT** as that.

HOT SPRINGS are found on **6 CONTINENTS —** all but **ANTARCTICA.**

There are **27,000** hot spring **SOURCES** in **JAPAN.**

The world's **LARGEST HOT SPRING** is in **New Zealand** and has a surface area of around **3.8 HECTARES** (9.3 acres).

At **CRYSTAL HOT SPRINGS** in **UTAH, USA**, **9.1 million litres** (2.4 million gallons) of **WATER** bring **400 tonnes** of **MINERALS** to the surface each day.

Over **100** wild **Japanese macaques** bathe in the alpine hot springs at **JIGOKUDANI MONKEY PARK** in Japan.

CHINA'S
3.5km-
(2.2 mile-) long **HUANGLONG ("YELLOW DRAGON") VALLEY** has more than
3,400
colourful natural **HOT SPRING POOLS** that look like a **DRAGON'S SCALES.**

The **MOTHER SPRING** in Colorado, USA, is the
DEEPEST
GEOTHERMAL HOT SPRING. It stretches down at least
305m
(1,002ft).

Hot springs flowing over **200m-** (650ft-) high cliffs in **TÜRKIYE** have created terraced white **CALCIUM FORMATIONS** known as the **Pamukkale Springs.**

The water reaching the surface at **HOT SPRINGS NATIONAL PARK** in **ARKANSAS, USA,** is rainwater that has been **UNDERGROUND** for
4,400 years.

Many **MICROORGANISMS** thrive in **HOT SPRINGS** and can give them vibrant colours. **ORANGE** *Phormidium* lives at up to **57°C** (135°F) while **GREEN** *Chloroflexus* can live in waters up to **85°C** (185°F).

Boiling Lake in Southern Dominica is a **VOLCANO-HYDROTHERMAL SPRING** that's almost literally boiling – the edges alone are
90°C (194°F).

PURE WATER
is a neutral **7pH,** but **HOT SPRING WATERS** can be **VERY ACIDIC** or **BASIC,** with pHs anywhere from
0.2–11.

At **113m** (370ft) across, Wyoming's **GRAND PRISMATIC SPRING** is the **BIGGEST** in the US.

TOP 10 LONGEST ERUPTIONS

YASUR • Vanuatu • Eruption: **780+ YEARS**

Continuous eruptions happen when a volcano is consistently active, with no more than a three-month gap between eruptions. Captain James Cook spotted Vanuatu's Mount Yasur spouting lava in 1774, but scientists estimate that it has been erupting continuously since the year 1240.

1

2 SANTA MARIA • Guatemala • Eruption: **102+ YEARS**

Located in the Sierra Madre mountains, this volcano has been erupting since 1922. Twenty years before that, in 1902, it had one of the biggest eruptions of the 20th century, producing a column of ash that shot up 28km (17 miles) into the sky.

3 DUKONO • Indonesia • Eruption: **91+ YEARS**

Indonesia's most active volcano, Dukono is one of several found on Halmahera Island. Its first recorded eruption was in 1550, and it has been spouting plumes of ash continuously since 1933.

4 STROMBOLI • Italy • Eruption: **91+ YEARS**

Mount Stromboli earned the nickname the "Lighthouse of the Mediterranean" due to its frequent eruptions over the past 2,000 years. The upper third of the volcano makes up an island off the coast of Sicily that is home to around 500 brave people.

5 SANGAY • Ecuador • Eruption: **77 YEARS**

This dramatic cone-like volcano is so tall, its peak is often covered with snow despite frequent eruptions. Sangay means "the frightener" in the language of the Quechua people.

6 AIRA • Japan • Eruption: **61 YEARS**

Aira is classed as a supervolcano because it once had a massive magnitude-8 eruption that gave it its current giant, cauldron-like shape. It remains one of Japan's most active volcanoes.

7 ERTA ALE • Ethiopia • Eruption: **57+ YEARS**

This low-lying shield volcano heats up the blazing hot desert around it with a lava lake, which first formed in 1902 and is the oldest-known lava lake on Earth.

8 EREBUS • Antarctica • Eruption: **52+ YEARS**

The southernmost active volcano on Earth, Erebus is found on the remote Ross Island off the western coast of Antarctica.

9 NYIRAGONGO • Democratic Republic of Congo • Eruption: **50 YEARS**

Located on a rift that runs through the Virunga Mountains, Nyiragongo rises 3,470m (11,385ft) and has a crater 2km (1 mile) across filled with one of the largest-known lava lakes.

10 ARENAL • Costa Rica • Eruption: **42 YEARS**

This young volcano is under 7,500 years old. It erupted continuously for 509 months straight, from 1968 to 2010, but is now dormant.

Unpredictable
VOLCANOES

A volcano is an opening in the surface of the planet. When it erupts, gas, ash, and boiling hot magma escape upwards from underneath the Earth's crust. Lava (magma outside a volcano) can destroy everything it flows over. But volcanoes also shape landscapes and bring valuable minerals to the surface.

About **10%** of people live in an area **DANGEROUSLY NEAR** an **ACTIVE VOLCANO.**

Around **75%** of the world's volcanoes are found in a **40,000KM-** (24,840 mile-) long horseshoe shape around the Pacific Ocean called the **"Ring of Fire".**

The **LARGEST VOLCANIC ERUPTION** in recorded history occured at **KIKAI-AKAHOYA,** near Japan. Around **7,300** YEARS AGO, it produced at least **300 CUBIC KM** (72 cubic miles) of material.

When **Krakatoa** erupted on a Pacific island in **1883,** it **RELEASED ENERGY** equivalent to a **200-MEGATONNE BOMB** and was heard **4,500KM** (2,800 miles) away in **AUSTRALIA.**

Destructive **ROCKS, ASH,** and **GAS** can flow from volcanoes at **725KPH** (450mph) – almost as fast as a **passenger jet.**

A **POWERFUL** volcanic eruption can **SHOOT ROCKS** **32KM** (20 miles) **INTO THE AIR.**

ERUPTIONS from volcanoes have created more than **80%** of the **SURFACE OF EARTH.**

The **1980** eruption of **MOUNT SAINT HELENS** in the US sent **VOLCANIC ASH** as far as **THE GREAT PLAINS,** **1,500KM** (930 miles) away.

At **9,170 m** (30,085ft) in height, **Mauna Loa** in **HAWAII**, USA, is the world's **TALLEST ACTIVE VOLCANO.**

Taal volcano in the **PHILIPPINES** is probably the **SMALLEST ACTIVE VOLCANO** in the world. At **311m** (1,020ft) tall, it's slightly shorter than the **EIFFEL TOWER** in Paris.

The **BIGGEST-KNOWN VOLCANO** in our Solar System isn't on Earth – **Olympus Mons** on **MARS** is an **AMAZING 600 km** (375 miles) **ACROSS.**

LAVA from a volcano can be as hot as **1,200°C** (2,200°F).

There are between **10** and **20 VOLCANIC ERUPTIONS** worldwide **EVERY DAY.**

Valuable
METALS

Metals are chemical elements or alloys (mixes of metallic elements) that can conduct heat and electricity relatively well. They are mostly found in rocks in Earth's crust, but only a few occur there in their pure form. The majority are mixed with other elements in chemical compounds. Metals are used to make many objects, and some can even be found in our bodies.

At least **94** of the **118** KNOWN CHEMICAL ELEMENTS are **metals** or have **METALLIC** properties.

The **3 metals** best at conducting **electricity** are **SILVER, COPPER,** and **GOLD.**

With a **MELTING POINT** of **−38.83°C** (-37.89˚F), **MERCURY** is the **ONLY METAL ELEMENT** that is **LIQUID** at room temperature.

The **LIGHTEST** metal is **lithium. A CUBIC CM** of lithium weighs just **0.534G** (0.3087oz per cubic in), about the same density as **PINE WOOD.**

The **HEAVIEST** metal is **osmium.** At **22.59G PER CUBIC CM** (13.06oz per cubic in), it is **TWICE** as heavy as **LEAD.**

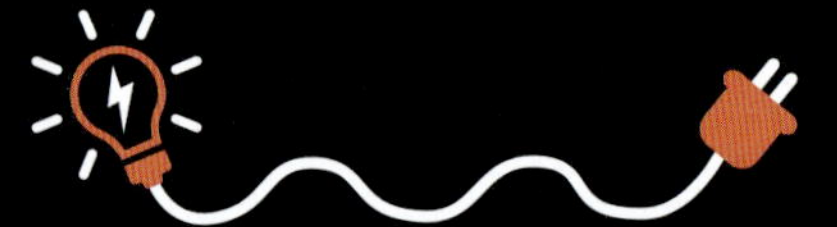

TITANIUM is as **STRONG AS STEEL** but **45% LIGHTER.** It is used to make aircraft parts and **MEDICAL IMPLANTS** for inside the body.

The **OLDEST-KNOWN** metal coin is the **Lydian lion,** made from **ELECTRUM** (a mix of gold and silver) in what is now **TÜRKIYE,** around **610** BCE.

31.1G (1 troy ounce) of **GOLD** can be beaten out to ultra-thin **GOLD-LEAF SHEETS** of **9 SQ M** (97 sq ft).

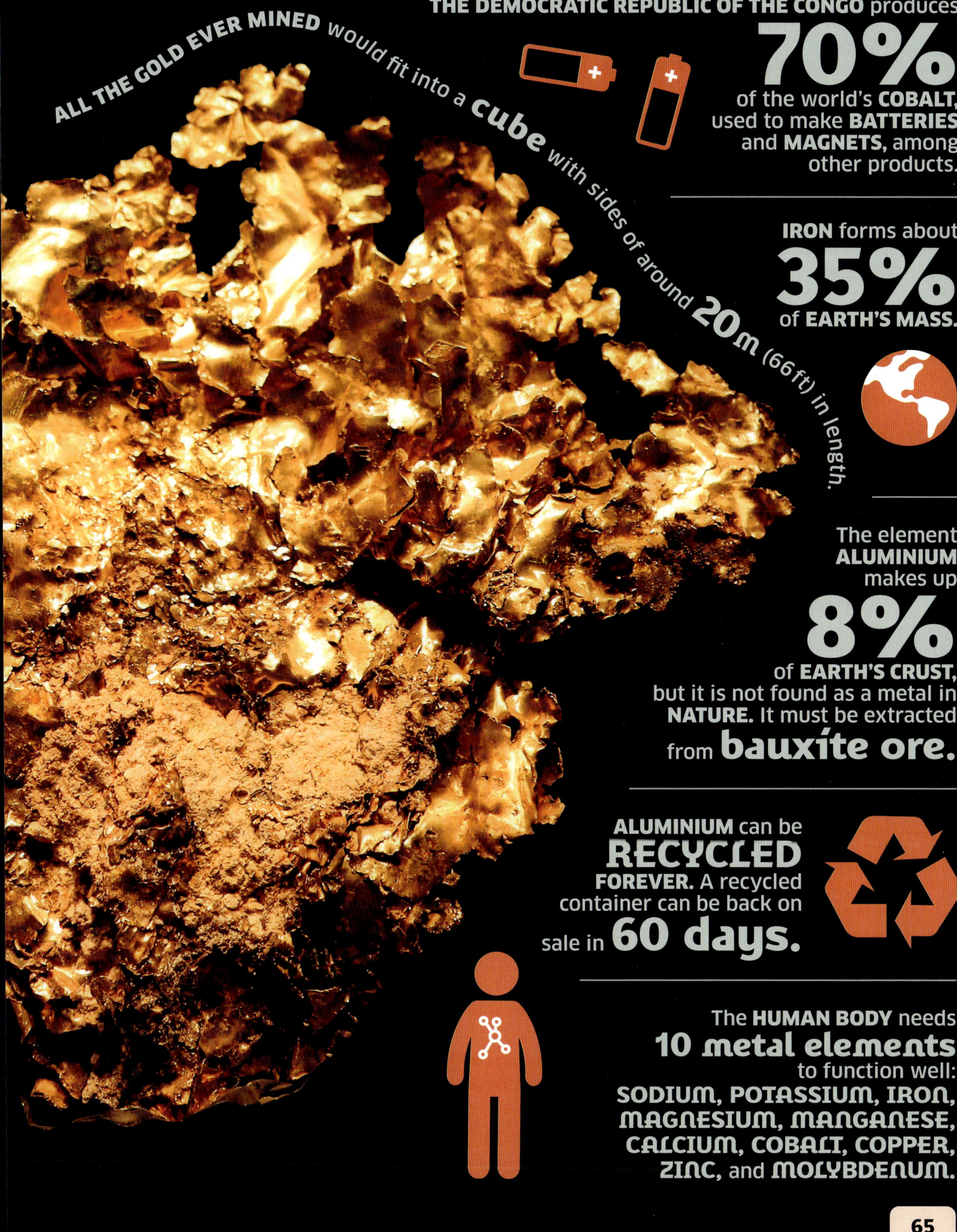

ALL THE GOLD EVER MINED would fit into a **cube** with sides of around **20 m** (66 ft) in length.

THE DEMOCRATIC REPUBLIC OF THE CONGO produces

70%
of the world's **COBALT**, used to make **BATTERIES** and **MAGNETS**, among other products.

IRON forms about

35%
of **EARTH'S MASS**

The element **ALUMINIUM** makes up

8%
of **EARTH'S CRUST**, but it is not found as a metal in **NATURE**. It must be extracted from **bauxite ore.**

ALUMINIUM can be **RECYCLED FOREVER**. A recycled container can be back on sale in **60 days.**

The **HUMAN BODY** needs **10 metal elements** to function well: **SODIUM, POTASSIUM, IRON, MAGNESIUM, MANGANESE, CALCIUM, COBALT, COPPER, ZINC,** and **MOLYBDENUM.**

Remarkable
ROCKS

Earth is a rocky planet. Rocks make up most of its crust and mantle. There are three main types: igneous, formed from cooled magma; sedimentary, formed when deposits of particles are compacted; and metamorphic, formed when existing rocks are transformed by great heat or pressure that changes their composition.

Rocks can be **TRANSFORMED** from one type to another through a **PROCESS** called the **ROCK CYCLE.** This takes **THOUSANDS** to **MILLIONS** of years.

The **OLDEST-KNOWN** rocks are found on the eastern shore of **HUDSON BAY, CANADA**, and have been dated at **4.28 BILLION YEARS OLD.**

90% of the **IGNEOUS ROCK** on Earth is **BASALT.** It makes up most of the rocky **OCEAN FLOOR.**

The **LARGEST BOULDER MOVED BY A GLACIER** is the Okotoks Erratic **"BIG ROCK"** in **ALBERTA, CANADA** – **10,000** to **12,000** years ago, the **16,500–tonne rock** was carried **HUNDREDS OF KILOMETRES.**

Giant's Causeway

in Northern Ireland contains around **40,000** 6-SIDED **BASALT COLUMNS** spread over **6KM** (4 miles).

Zero places on Earth

have a **COMPLETE SEQUENCE OF ROCKS** that span from the **PRECAMBRIAN PERIOD TO TODAY.**

Metamorphic

ROCKS are formed at temperatures over

200°C
(392°F).

The **TALLEST VOLCANIC ROCK COLUMNS** on Earth are found in **Devils Tower,** a striking monolith in **WYOMING, USA,** that is **264m** (867ft) in height.

With their **EMBEDDED CRYSTALS** and **CAPTIVATING PATTERNS,** **METAMORPHIC ROCKS** are often used for epic architecture projects, such as the **73m-** (240ft-) high **TAJ MAJAL.**

The rocks in **EARTH'S CRUST** are almost entirely made up of just **8 ELEMENTS:** oxygen, silicon, iron, aluminium, calcium, magnesium, sodium, and potassium.

METAMORPHIC ROCKS form deep in the **EARTH'S CRUST,** up to **35KM** (22 miles) **BELOW THE SURFACE.**

SEDIMENTARY ROCKS found in the **ISUA GREENSTONE BELT** in Greenland date from **3.8 BILLION YEARS AGO** and may contain chemical evidence of **EARLY LIFE.**

Coal is a **SEDIMENTARY** rock made from **FOSSILIZED PLANTS** that were buried about **300 million** years ago.

Possibly the **LIGHTEST** rock on Earth is **PUMICE,** a volcanic stone full of air bubbles. It can **FLOAT ON WATER** for at least **20 YEARS.**

73% of the rocks found on **EARTH'S SURFACE** are **SEDIMENTARY,** yet this type only makes up about **8%** of the **CRUST.**

The largest **ammonite** fossil, the shell of an **EXTINCT MARINE CEPHALOPOD**, measures **1.8 m** (6ft) in diameter.

FOSSILS from more than **6,000 HUMAN INDIVIDUALS** have been discovered.

The largest **FOSSILIZED BONE** is a **2.4 m** (8ft) **titanosaur THIGHBONE** found in **ARGENTINA**.

The **EARLIEST human** (*Homo sapien*) fossils, found in **MOROCCO**, are more than **315,000 YEARS OLD.**

The **HUMAN ANCESTORS** called *Denisovans* are only known from fossils of **3 TEETH, 1 FINGER BONE,** part of a **JAW,** and a few **BONE CHIPS.**

A fossilized ***T. rex* skull** weighs over **72 KG** (160lb), about the same as a **WASHING MACHINE.**

The remains of **4,000 dire wolves** and **2,000 sabre-toothed cats** have been found in the **LA BREA TAR PITS** in **LOS ANGELES, USA.**

The **LARGEST FOSSILIZED SHARK TEETH** belong to the **megalodon.** They measure up to **17.8 cm** (6⁹⁄₁₀in) long, the length of a **BANANA.**

The **SHANDONG FOSSIL BONE BEDS** in **CHINA** is one of the most productive sites for **DINOSAUR FOSSILS. 7,600** of them were unearthed there in just **7 MONTHS** from a **300M** (980ft) pit.

The **DEEPEST** fossil ever found, a **PLATEOSAUR KNUCKLEBONE,** was dug up from **2.3 KM** (1⅖ miles) **UNDER THE SEABED** by an oil-rig drill near **NORWAY.**

FOSSILS

Fossils give us a glimpse of ancient life. They can form when a plant or animal is quickly buried under mud or sediment. Over time more layers of sediment pile up and turn to rock while water seeps into the remains, replacing them with minerals. Erosion helps buried fossils resurface for us to discover.

Fossils are the **REMAINS** or traces of **LIVING THINGS** from more than **10,000** – often **MILLIONS OF** – years ago.

The **OLDEST** fossils are of **stromatolites,** structures left by bacteria about **3.48 billion** years ago.

Fossilization is **RARE.** Fossils probably tell us about less than **1%** of all the species to have lived.

50,000

-YEAR-OLD FOSSILS of **HUMAN POO,** or **COPROLITES,** show **PREHISTORIC HUMANS** ate meat, berries, nuts, and vegetables.

The most **EXPENSIVE** fossil sold at auction was an almost complete **STEGOSAURUS,** nicknamed "Apex". It sold for **£34.1 million** in **2024.**

FOSSILS of **450-million-year-old MARINE CREATURES** have been found at the top of **QOMOLANGMA FENG (MOUNT EVEREST), 8,849 m** (29,031ft) above sea level.

Amazing MINERALS

Minerals are solid, non-living materials that occur naturally. Rocks are made up of minerals, which are formed of two or more chemical elements. Some minerals are treasured as gemstones, including some of the hardest and most expensive materials on Earth.

More than **90%** of **EARTH'S CRUST** is made up of **silicate MINERALS,** containing **SILICON** and **OXYGEN.**

There are over **6,000** **"SPECIES"** of **MINERAL,** but only **100** are **COMMON.**

Granite is formed deep below Earth's surface. It always contains at least **2 MINERALS, FELDSPAR** and **QUARTZ.**

A **SILICATE** called **bridgmanite** is Earth's most **COMMON MINERAL,** accounting for about **38%** of its **TOTAL VOLUME.**

The first sample of **BRIDGMANITE** was taken from a **meteorite** that **HIT EARTH** in **1879,** but it was only recognized as a **MINERAL** in **2014.**

HUMANS need to **CONSUME SMALL AMOUNTS** of **16 DIFFERENT MINERALS,** such as **PHOSPHORUS** and **CHLORIDE,** to stay **HEALTHY.**

Diamond is the **HARDEST-KNOWN** mineral, **RATED 10** on the **MOHS HARDNESS SCALE.** It is **58 times** harder than **CORUNDUM,** the next-hardest mineral.

The **softest** mineral is claylike **TALC,** often used in **COSMETICS,** with a **MOHS SCALE RATING OF 1.**

There are **315** **MINERALS** that are treasured as **gemstones,** with just **4** considered **"PRECIOUS":** **DIAMOND, RUBY, EMERALD,** and **SAPPHIRE.**

The **MASS** of **GEMSTONES** is measured in **CARATS.** **ONE CARAT** equals **0.2**G (0.007oz).

In **2016,** a **12-carat** **BLUE DIAMOND,** the **BLUE MOON OF JOSEPHINE,** sold at auction for **£36.2 million.**

After **BLUE DIAMONDS, jadeite** is the most **EXPENSIVE MINERAL,** at around **£2.3 million** PER CARAT.

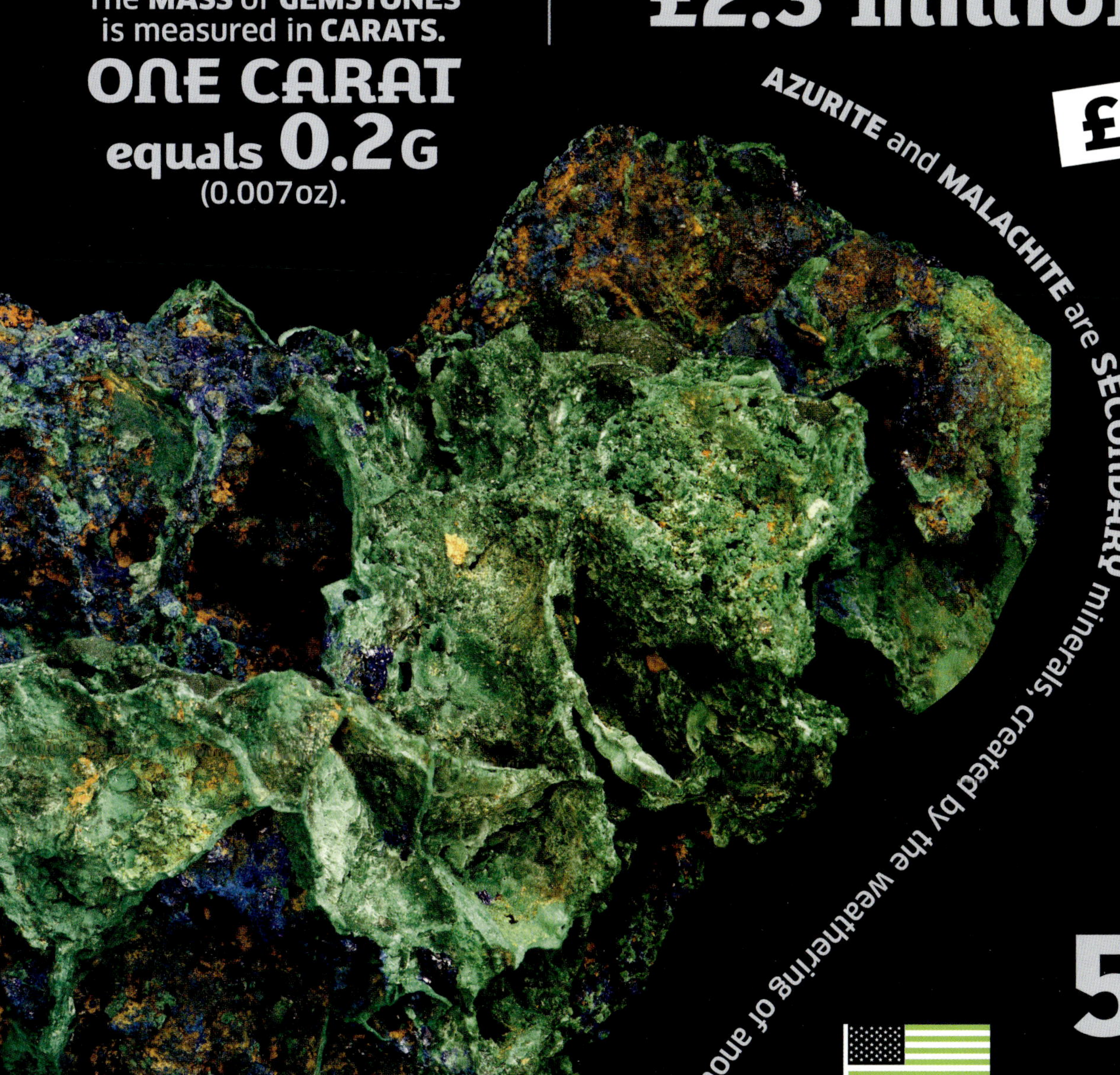

Earth's **rarest** mineral is **KYAWTHUITE.** Only **1 crystal** of this **DUSKY-ORANGE** gemstone has ever been found, in **MYANMAR.**

About **54%** of all minerals are **NAMED AFTER PEOPLE,** most after those involved in their discovery but some after historical figures, such as the composer **MOZART** and astronaut **NEIL ARMSTRONG.**

When an **ELECTRIC CURRENT** is passed through a **quartz crystal,** it vibrates **33,768 TIMES A SECOND.** This precise rate of vibration can be used to **KEEP TIME.**

There are **6,100 RECOGNIZED MINERALS** on Earth, all of which have a **CRYSTAL STRUCTURE.**

The **OLDEST-KNOWN** pieces of **EARTH'S CRUST** are **4.4–BILLION–YEAR–OLD ZIRCON CRYSTALS** found on a **SHEEP RANCH** in **WESTERN AUSTRALIA.**

Tiny **APATITE CRYSTALS** make up around **65%** of the weight of **HUMAN BONES.**

ALL CRYSTALS display one of **219** SYMMETRICAL FORMS.

CRYSTALS

Crystals are minerals made up of atoms arranged in a repeated 3-D lattice pattern. On the outside, this gives crystals a geometric shape with many flat faces. Some crystals are tiny, such as those of salt or gold, but if there is enough space, they can grow into giant formations that fill entire caves.

An **18M-** (59ft-) long **BLOCK OF BERYL** found in **MADAGASCAR** is the **WORLD'S LARGEST-KNOWN CRYSTAL.** It weighs about **380 TONNES.**

Each mineral has a unique **TEMPERATURE RANGE** at which it will crystallize. **Olivine,** for example, crystallizes out of **COOLING MAGMA** at **1,300−1,200°C** (2400–2200°F).

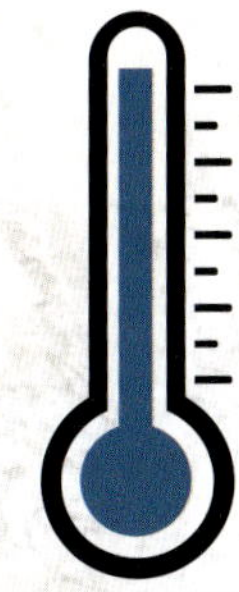

In the year **2000**, a huge **CAVE OF CRYSTALS,** filled with crystals up to **11m** (36ft) long, was discovered by miners **290m** (1,000ft) below **NAICA MOUNTAIN** in Mexico.

Over **500 types** **OF CRYSTAL** are **fluorescent,** glowing under **ULTRAVIOLET LIGHT,** including the property's namesake, **FLUORITE.**

The **LARGEST CRYSTALS** at **NAICA** may have taken **1 million years** to form, growing by an amount equal to **THIS PAGE'S THICKNESS** every **200 YEARS.**

Pyrite, or **FOOL'S GOLD,** forms crystals as **PERFECT CUBES** up to **9.5KG** (21lb) in weight.

BLUE PLANET

Unbelievable
OCEANS

There are five named oceans around the world – the Atlantic, Pacific, Arctic, Indian, and Southern. All these massive bodies of salt water are connected in one global ocean that covers most of our planet.

There are more than **250,000** known **MARINE SPECIES** in our oceans.

The **OCEAN** likely began to appear around **3.8 billion** years ago, when the **AIR COOLED** to below the boiling point of water, **100°C** (212°F).

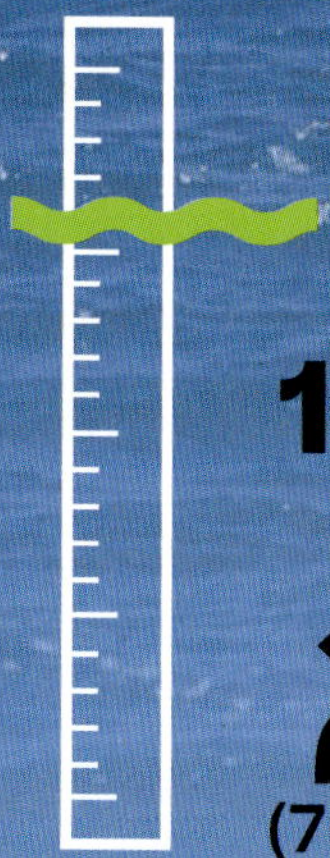

SEA LEVELS change over time. They may have been at their **HIGHEST** **117 million** years ago, when levels were **200 m** (700ft) above today's.

Life began in the ocean, which today accounts for **90%** of Earth's **HABITABLE SPACE.**

The **OCEAN** spans **71%** of **EARTH'S SURFACE** and has **96.5%** of its **WATER.**

The ocean's **STRONGEST CURRENT** is the **ANTARCTIC CIRCUMPOLAR** current, which moves **130 million** cubic m (4.6 billion cubic ft) of water per second.

If the **OCEAN EVAPORATED,** it would leave a **layer of salt 166 m** (500ft) **THICK** covering the **ENTIRE** Earth.

There are **5 MAJOR GYRES** (circular ocean currents), caused by the wind, arrangement of continents, and Earth's rotation.

Scientists estimate that a mere **9%** of all **MARINE SPECIES** have been named.

The **INDIAN OCEAN** is the **WARMEST,** reaching temperatures of **28°C** (82°F) in **SUMMER.**

The global ocean averages **3,682 m** (12,080ft) **DEEP.** The Pacific is the **DEEPEST PART,** with an average depth of **4,280 m** (14,040ft).

39% of the **OCEAN** is considered to be "**national waters**", associated with **PARTICULAR COUNTRIES.**

The **PACIFIC** is the **LARGEST** named ocean. At **165,250,000 SQ KM** (63,800,000 sq miles), it's **2 TIMES** the size of the **ATLANTIC.**

IN TOTAL, the ocean contains about **1.34 billion CUBIC KM** (321 million cubic miles) of **WATER.**

Viruses are the most common **BIOLOGICAL ENTITIES** in the ocean – **1 mL** (⅕ tsp) **OF SEAWATER** contains up to **10 million** of them.

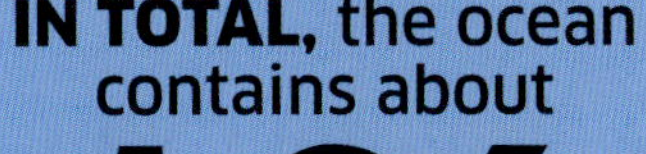

Frosty
FROZEN SEAS

Sea ice can be found in the Arctic and Antarctic in sub-zero temperatures. It starts as small crystals, before forming plates of ice that freeze together. The area of ocean frozen over varies with the seasons and the changing climate.

Sea waves can create circular **pancake ice,** with discs up to **3m** (10ft) in **DIAMETER.**

When the **SEA ICE** reaches around **4m** (13ft) thick, the sea below is **SEALED OFF** from the air above.

There are **3 SPECIES OF WHALE** that **STAY IN THE ARCTIC** all year round. The **LARGEST** is the **bowhead whale,** which can weigh up to **90 TONNES.**

When the **ARCTIC ICE** melts, **polar bears** have to **SWIM TOWARDS LAND.** They can cover **160km** (100 miles) of water in **ONE GO.**

Ice algae, the base of the **ARCTIC FOOD CHAIN,** grows bountifully in the **LOWER 5cm** (2in) of sea ice, with **HUGE BLOOMS** of it in **SPRING** that disperse into the sea as the ice melts.

As soon as the **SUN RETURNS** after the Arctic winter, **ICE ALGAE** start to **GROW,** even in conditions with **0.1%** of the **LIGHT** found on **THE SURFACE.**

The changing sea ice around **Antarctica** has recently varied between **1.8 million** SQ KM (700,000 sq miles) in the **SUMMER** and **20.2 million** SQ KM (7.8 million sq miles) in the **WINTER.**

Summer sea ice in the **ARCTIC OCEAN** is declining by **13%** every **10 YEARS,** so there might be **ICE-FREE SUMMERS BEFORE 2050.**

SEPTEMBER 2012 saw the **LOWEST** recorded amount of **SEA ICE** in the **ARCTIC OCEAN,** with **3.4 million** SQ KM (1.3 million sq miles), which is about the size of **INDIA.**

A **POLAR BEAR** can **HEAR** and **SMELL** amazingly well. When hunting, it can detect a **seal's lair** beneath **2 m** (6 ft 7 in) of sea ice.

SALT DOES NOT FREEZE, so ice crystals expel it into the water. After **1 year,** sea ice contains **ALMOST NO SALT.**

From **SPACE, ANTARCTICA** appears to be **twice AS BIG** in **WINTER** as it is in the **SUMMER,** due to the growth of **sea ice** surrounding it.

Seawater starts FREEZING around −1.9°C (28.5°F).

Rolling
RIVERS

A river flows over land, carrying fresh water from its source to its mouth, such as a lake or sea. The water is fresh because it contains less than 1 per cent salt – perfect for drinking, agriculture, and industry. Powerful rivers can erode (wear away) rock, changing the landscape to create valleys and canyons.

Rivers only contain about **0.006%** of all our planet's **FRESH WATER.**

The Amazon basin contains about **38%** of Earth's **RIVER WATER.**

In **2007**, Slovenian **MARTIN STREL** swam the entire **5,268 KM** (3,273 miles) length of the **Amazon River.** He was in the water for **10 hours A DAY FOR 66 days.**

At least **260** different **SPECIES OF FISH** live in the **MISSISSIPPI RIVER.** That's **25%** of all the **FISH SPECIES** that can be found **IN THE US.**

The **AMAZON** is the world's **WIDEST RIVER.** It can reach **48 KM** (30 miles) across in the **WET SEASON.** It also has the **MOST TRIBUTARIES – 1,100.**

PATAGONIA has 3 large glacial rivers fed by melting ice.

The **LONGEST UNDERGROUND RIVER** is in **MEXICO** – it winds under the **YUCATÁN PENINSULA** for **153 KM** (95 miles).

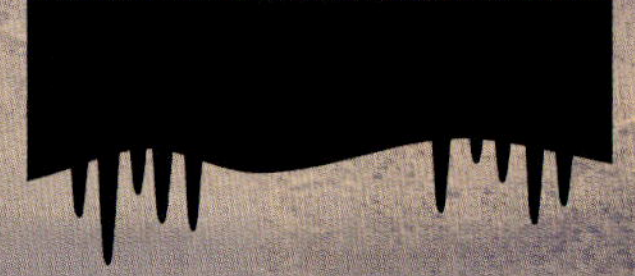

The deepest river is the **CONGO RIVER** in Africa. It can reach

220 m

(722ft), about the **HEIGHT** of a **TOWER** on the **GOLDEN GATE BRIDGE.**

COLOMBIA'S Caño Crístales is known as the **"RIVER OF 5 COLOURS"** because plants make the water look bright **YELLOW, GREEN, RED, BLUE,** and **BLACK.**

Europe's **DANUBE BASIN** is the most *international* **RIVER SYSTEM,** flowing through **19 COUNTRIES.**

The **LONGEST-KNOWN** river not on Earth is the

412 KM-

(256 mile-) long **VID FLUMINA** on Saturn's moon **TITAN –** it contains **LIQUID METHANE** instead of water.

Part of **CHINA'S SECOND-LONGEST** river, the **Huang He** (Yellow River), **DRIED UP** for a record **226 DAYS IN A ROW** in 1997.

THE NILE in **AFRICA** is the world's **LONGEST** river. It is at least

6,650 KM

(4,132 miles) **LONG,** which is more than

½ of **EARTH'S DIAMETER!**

A moderately fast river **FLOWS** at around

5—6 KPH

(3-4mph), a walking pace, but can reach **SPEEDS** of more than **24 KPH** (15mph) during a flood.

THE OKAVANGO RIVER in southern Africa forms a **RARE INLAND DELTA** in Botswana with more than **150,000 ISLANDS.**

Despite the risk of **FLOODING,** around **450 million PEOPLE LIVE** on river deltas.

Estuaries are considered the **"nurseries of the sea",** where **75%** of **CAUGHT FISH** begin their lives.

When the tide rises in Britain's **SEVERN ESTUARY,** it can cause a tidal bore with a series of waves nearly **2 m** (7 ft) high, moving about **21 KPH** (13 mph), that surfers can ride on.

The world's **LONGEST** estuary is the **GULF OF OB** in northern Russia. It's **885 KM** (550 miles) **LONG** and a **MIGRATION ROUTE** for **beluga whales.**

The **Mekong Delta** in **VIETNAM** is also known as the **"NINE DRAGONS DELTA"** as the river splits into **9 SERPENT-SHAPED STREAMS.**

MANGROVES, which grow in **118 COUNTRIES,** are the **ONLY TYPE OF TREE** that can **survive in salt water. 68%** of **MANGROVE FORESTS** are found in deltas and estuaries.

The world's **LONGEST** river, **the Nile,** ends in a delta in Egypt that is **250 KM** (155 miles) **WIDE.**

Around **½** of Egypt's **POPULATION** lives in the **NILE DELTA REGION.**

The **LARGEST DELTA** on Earth is where the **GANGES** and **BRAHMAPUTRA** rivers reach the coast in **BANGLADESH** and **WEST BENGAL, INDIA.** It covers about **106,000 SQ KM** (41,000 sq miles).

The UK's **Thames Estuary** is home to the **LONDON ARRAY,** an offshore wind farm, with **175 WIND TURBINES.**

ESTUARIES AND DELTAS

Deltas are fan-shaped areas of built-up sediment where a river splits into smaller channels as it meets the sea, a lake, or another river. If a river flows slowly into the sea, seawater may push into the river mouth and form an estuary where fresh water mixes with salt water.

Most of today's deltas have formed since sea levels became relatively stable, around **8,000 years ago.**

The **YUKON DELTA** spans 4,100km (2,550 miles) of coast with **22 RIVER MOUTHS.**

The **DANUBE DELTA** in **EASTERN EUROPE** is home to around **2,000** PLANT and **5,000** ANIMAL SPECIES.

North America's **ST LAWRENCE RIVER** estuary connects to the Great Lakes, draining around **25%** of the world's surface fresh water into the Atlantic.

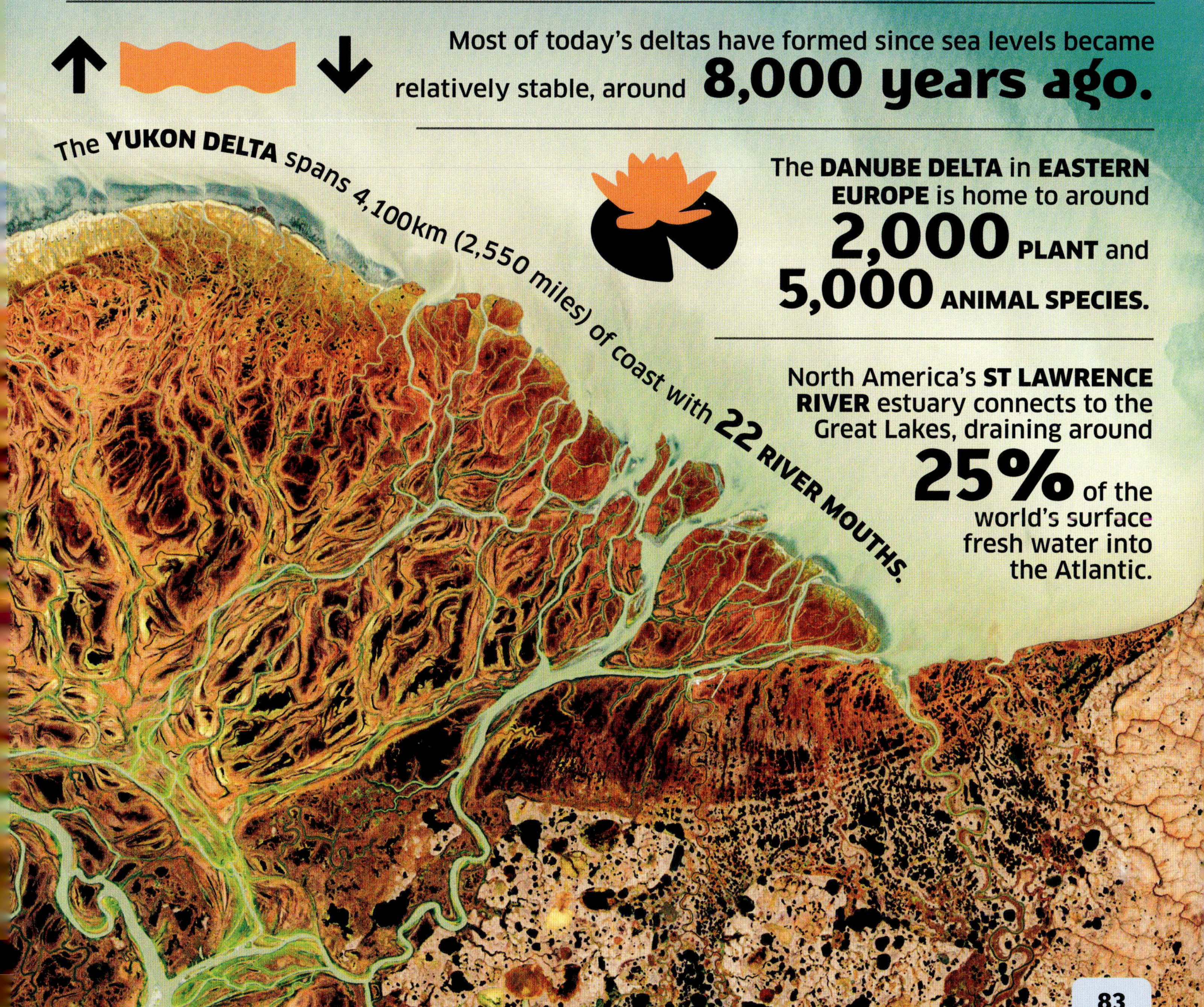

The **LARGEST WAVE** recorded on a **GREAT LAKE** was **8.8 m** (28.8ft) high.

South America's **BIGGEST** lake, **TITICACA**, is also the **HIGHEST** major lake on Earth, found **3,810 m** (12,500ft) above sea level.

There are more than **6,000** **shipwrecks** at the bottom of North America's **Great Lakes.**

Siberia's **LAKE BAIKAL** contains the **MOST WATER** of any freshwater lake – more water than **ALL 5** of North America's **GREAT LAKES** put together.

The **SALTIEST** lake is **Gaet'ale Pond** in **ETHIOPIA**. Its water contains **43.3%** salt by weight. The global ocean has an average of **3.4%**.

At **1,642 m** (1 mile) deep, **LAKE BAIKAL,** formed in a rift valley in **SIBERIA**, is by far the world's **DEEPEST** freshwater lake.

THE GREAT LAKES are fed by around **5,000** tributaries.

GHANA'S **Lake Volta,** contained by the **AKOSOMBO DAM**, is the **LARGEST ARTIFICIAL LAKE.** It covers **8,502** **SQ KM** (3,283 sq miles), which is **7 TIMES** the size of **LOS ANGELES.**

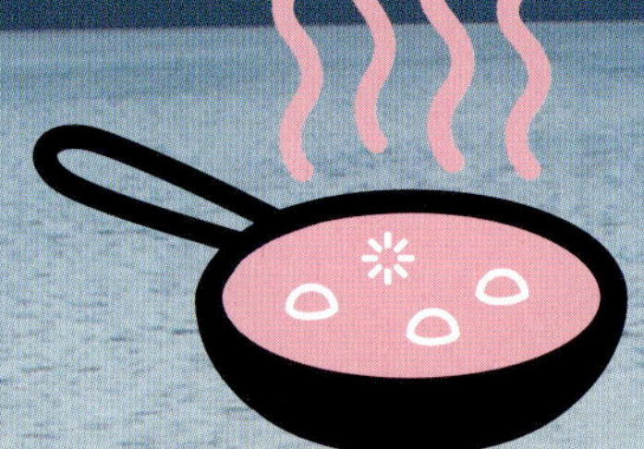

NEW ZEALAND'S **Frying Pan Lake** is the world's **LARGEST HOT SPRING** – the **ACIDIC** water's temperature stays a toasty **50–60°C** (122–140°F).

The world's **LONGEST** lake is **AFRICA'S LAKE TANGANYIKA.** It's **673 KM** (418 miles) **LONG** but is only **16 KM** (10 miles) **WIDE** at some points.

There are more than **1,000 species** in Lake Tanganyika that **AREN'T FOUND ANYWHERE ELSE.**

LAKES

Lakes are simply areas of water surrounded by land. They are formed in different ways, including by glaciers melting, volcano craters filling up with water, or even beavers building dams! People also build artificial lakes to hold water supplies or generate electricity by hydroelectric power.

About **70%** of the planet's lake water can be found in **3 continents — NORTH AMERICA, AFRICA,** and **ASIA.**

There are at least

304 million lakes on Earth.

Kenya's **LAKE BOGORIA** is the feeding ground for up to **2 MILLION** flamingos.

Lake Superior, on the border of the **US** and **CANADA,** is the **LARGEST FRESHWATER LAKE** by surface area. It contains **10%** of the fresh water found on Earth's surface.

Only **20 lakes** on Earth are more than **1 million YEARS OLD.**

The number of **GLACIAL LAKES** increased by **53%** from 1990–2018.

Often called the **LARGEST LAKE FISH,** the **BELUGA STURGEON 7 m** (23ft) **LONG** and **WEIGH 1,570 KG** (3,460lb).

TOP 10
BIGGEST LAKES

CASPIAN SEA • Between Europe and Asia •
Surface area: **371,000 SQ KM** (143,000 sq miles)

1

This inland sea is technically Earth's largest lake. Cut off from the ocean around 11 million years ago, it contains about a third of the world's inland surface water.

2 **LAKE SUPERIOR** • Canada and USA •
Surface area: **82,100 SQ KM** (31,700 sq miles)

Superior is the largest of North America's five Great Lakes, containing half of the total amount of water in them. It is fed by around 200 tributaries (rivers).

3 **LAKE VICTORIA** • Africa • Surface area: **68,870 SQ KM** (25,590 sq miles)

Lake Victoria is Africa's biggest lake and the largest tropical lake on Earth. Its basin spans three countries and is dotted with islands and reefs.

4 **LAKE HURON** • Canada and USA • Surface area: **59,600 SQ KM** (23,000 sq miles)

Lake Huron has the longest shoreline of any of the Great Lakes and contains the largest freshwater island, which itself has 100 lakes on it.

5 **LAKE MICHIGAN** • USA • Surface area: **58,000 SQ KM** (22,000 sq miles)

The name of this freshwater lake comes from the Ojibwe word for "big lake", which is "michigami". Its scenic shores boast the world's largest freshwater system of sand dunes.

6 **LAKE TANGANYIKA** • Africa • Surface area: **32,600 SQ KM** (12,600 sq miles)

Lake Tanganyika in eastern Africa is the longest freshwater lake on the planet at 660km (410 miles). It makes up the boundary between the Democratic Republic of the Congo and Tanzania.

7 **BAIKAL** • Russia • Surface area: **31,500 SQ KM** (12,200 sq miles)

At roughly 25 million years old, Siberia's Lake Baikal is the world's oldest freshwater lake in existence. Over 330 rivers and streams flow into the lake, which is the deepest on Earth.

8 **GREAT BEAR LAKE** • Canada • Surface area: **31,000 SQ KM** (12,000 sq miles)

Named after the bears that live along its shores, this lake in the Northwest Territories reaches into the Arctic Circle.

9 **MALAWI** • Africa • Surface area: **29,500 SQ KM** (11,400 sq miles)

Up to 1,000 species of fish live in this freshwater lake, and more than 56,000 fishers are employed here. It produces 100,000 tonnes of fish per year, but climate change and pollution put its fish stocks at risk.

10 **GREAT SLAVE LAKE** • Canada • Surface area: **27,000 SQ KM** (10,000 sq miles)

The second-largest lake that is completely within Canadian borders, Great Slave Lake is North America's deepest at 600m (2,000ft).

Shifting
TIDES

Tides are the rise and fall of the sea that happens twice a day on most coasts. They are caused by the Moon's gravity pulling on Earth's oceans, creating bulges in the water. Tides are a type of slow-moving wave, with high tides happening at each crest.

Most coasts have **SEMI-DIURNAL TIDES**, meaning there are **2 HIGH** and **2 LOW** tides every **24 HOURS AND 50 MINUTES.**

It takes **6 hours and 12.5 minutes** for the water at the shore to move from **high** to **low tide** or vice versa.

The gravity of the **SUN** also affects tides, but its force is only **46%** of that of the **MOON.**

The **DIFFERENCE** between the **WATER LEVEL** at high and low tide is called the **TIDAL RANGE.** The average tidal range in the open ocean is **0.6 m** (2ft).

CANADA'S Bay of Fundy has the **HIGHEST TIDAL RANGE** on Earth: **16 m** (53ft).

In some places with a tidal range of at least **6 m** (20ft), a **STRONG WAVE** called a **TIDAL BORE** pushes against the current up a **RIVER MOUTH.**

There are about **3 terawatts** of power in the ocean's tides. That's about the same as the world's **DAILY ENERGY CONSUMPTION.**

The **TIDAL CURRENT** in **Saltstraumen Maelstrom** in **NORWAY** reaches **37KPH** (28mph), one of the **STRONGEST** in the world.

The **SIHWA LAKE TIDAL POWER STATION** in **SOUTH KOREA** produces **552.7 GIGAWATT HOURS** of energy annually – enough for **500,000 people.**

About **100 TIDAL BORES** exist worldwide. About **1/5** of them are in the **UK.**

A **NEAP TIDE** occurs **twice** a month when the tidal range is at its **LOWEST.**

A **SPRING TIDE** occurs **twice** a month when the tidal range is at its **HIGHEST.**

The **SUN'S GRAVITATIONAL PULL** affects the tides, although it's **390 times** further away from the Earth than is the **MOON.**

The **QIANTANG RIVER** in **HANGZHOU, CHINA,** has the **world's largest tidal bore.** A **9m-** (30ft-) **HIGH** tidal wave roars up the river.

A few coasts, such as on the **GULF OF MEXICO,** have **DIURNAL TIDES** with just **1 high** and **1 low tide** every **24 HOURS** and **50 MINUTES,** or **1 LUNAR DAY.**

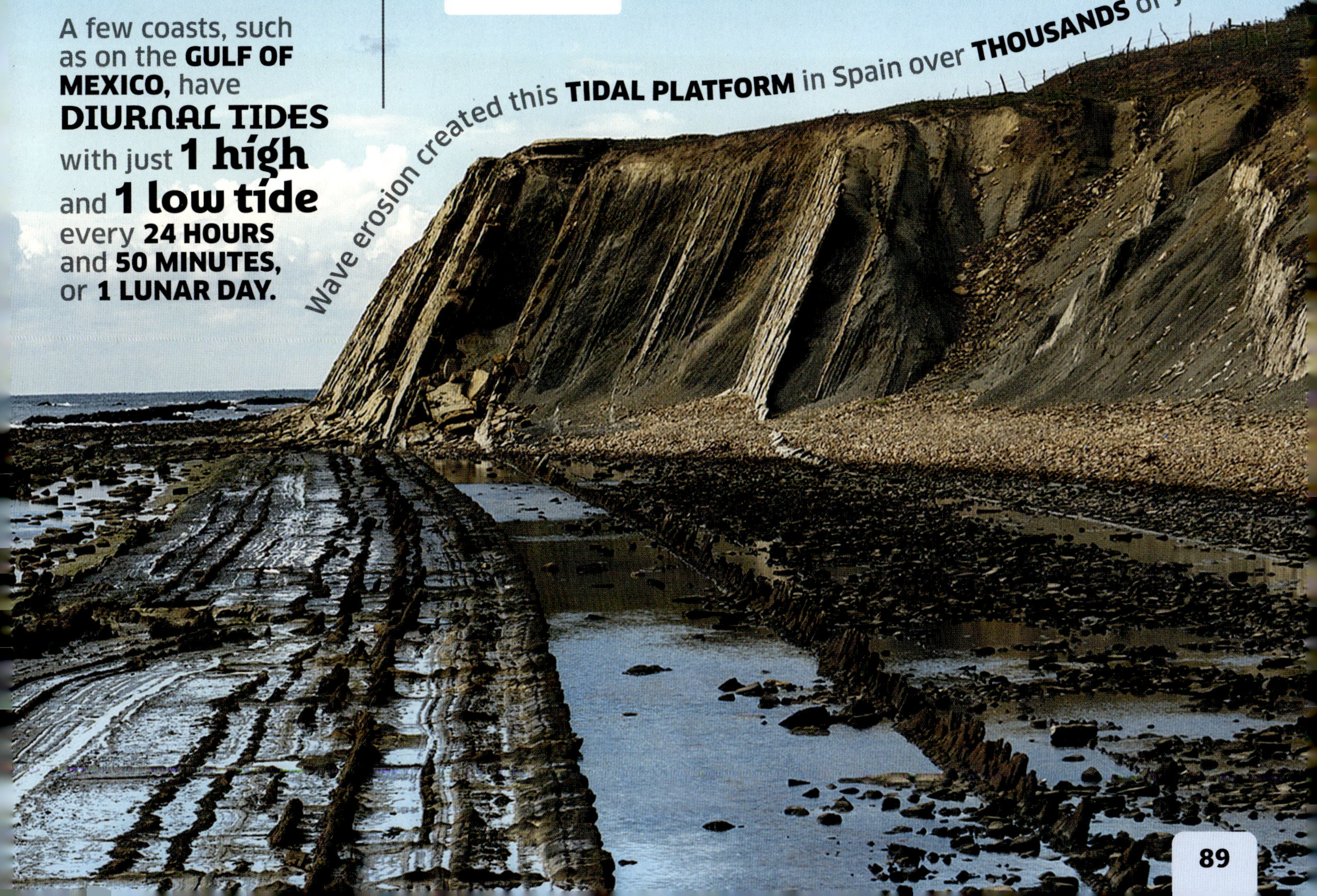

Wonderful WAVES

Waves on the ocean surface are usually made by wind – although gravity, earthquakes, and landslides under the water can cause them, too. The speed of the wind, how long it lasts, and the area it covers affect a wave's size. Big ones can shape coastal landscapes and even power our homes.

The **HIGHEST OPEN-WATER WAVE** measured by a **BUOY** was **19 m** (62.3ft) tall in the **ATLANTIC OCEAN** in 2013.

No **2 waves ARE IDENTICAL** – each one is **UNIQUE.**

Waves don't just happen on the surface. **INTERNAL WAVES** form underwater, reaching down as far as **200 m** (650ft).

Some **PACIFIC WAVES** that reach the coast of **CALIFORNIA, USA,** are thought to have **TRAVELLED** more than **8,000 KM** (4,970 miles) over **10 DAYS.**

SEA WAVES caused by **WIND** have **WAVELENGTHS** (the distance between consecutive crests) of **90—180 m** (300–600ft).

For **SURFACE WAVES,** the time between **WAVE CRESTS** is around **5—20 SECONDS.** For **TSUNAMIS,** it can be **2 hours!**

TSUNAMIS are giant waves caused by underwater **EARTHQUAKES, LANDSLIDES,** and **ERUPTIONS.** They come up from the ocean floor and have **WAVELENGTHS** of **500–1,000 KM** (300–600 miles).

STORM WAVES moved a **630-tonne boulder** (about the **WEIGHT** of **4 MALE BLUE WHALES**) more than **2.5 M** (8.2ft) across an **IRISH CLIFFTOP** over **1 WINTER.**

The **DEADLIEST** tsunami on record took place in the **INDIAN OCEAN** on **26 DECEMBER 2004,** killing **230,000** people.

WIND WAVES travel around **8—55 KPH** (5–35mph), but **MONSTER TSUNAMIS** can reach **965 KPH** (600mph), as **FAST** as a **JET.**

The world's first commercial **WAVE FARM** opened in 2008, **5 KM** (3.1 miles) off the coast of **PORTUGAL,** generating **2.25 MEGAWATTS** of **ELECTRICITY** at a time.

In **1 YEAR, WAVE POWER** could produce enough **ENERGY** to supply **ELECTRICITY** for **EUROPE** – almost **10 times over!**

The **TALLEST WAVE** ever **SURFED** was **30.9 m** (101ft) **HIGH** off the **PORTUGUESE COAST** by **ANTÓNIO LAUREANO** in 2020.

In **2013,** Frenchman **CAMILLE JUBAN** **windsurfed** a **SINGLE WAVE** for **7 minutes** and **3 SECONDS** – a **WORLD RECORD.**

A wave **BREAKS** when it reaches shallow water with a depth that is **1.3 times** its height.

Intriguing
ISLANDS

Islands are pieces of land that are completely surrounded by water. They can be formed in many ways. For instance, undersea volcanic eruptions can build up into mountains that break the surface, or erosion by flowing water can cut off part of the mainland. Tectonic plates may push up bits of land, and ancient coral reefs can even grow into marine islands.

Found in the **ARCTIC**, the **WORLD'S LARGEST ISLAND**, **Greenland,** is **3 TIMES** the size of **TEXAS.**

At **388 SQ KM** (150 sq miles), **KIRITIMATI ATOLL** is the **largest island** made **ENTIRELY** of **CORAL.**

Around **9%** of **PEOPLE LIVE ON ISLANDS.**

The most **REMOTE INHABITED ARCHIPELAGO** (group of islands) is **Tristan da Cunha,** which is **2,800 KM** (1,750 miles) east from the nearest landmass, **SOUTH AFRICA.**

Islands tend to be **YOUNG** in terms of geological time. The **OLDEST, MADAGASCAR,** dates to around **88 million years ago** when it broke off from **INDIA.**

More than **80%** of **PLANTS** and **ANIMALS** on **Madagascar** are found nowhere else in the world.

India's **LOHACHARA ISLAND,** once home to **6,000 people,** completely **DISAPPEARED** due to **FLOODING** in **1996.**

An island **100 m** (300ft) across suddenly appeared off the coast of **JAPAN** in **OCTOBER 2023** following **UNDERSEA ERUPTIONS.** It disappeared again in **MARCH 2024.**

With more than **150 million** residents, **JAVA** is the island with the **BIGGEST POPULATION.**

HUB ISLAND, off New York, is the world's **SMALLEST INHABITED ISLAND,** with room for just one house. At around **307 SQ M** (3,330 sq ft), the single-family residence is about the size of a **tennis court.**

Sweden is the country with the **MOST ISLANDS –** **267,570** of them.

LOKRUM ISLAND (pictured) is a Mediterranean **NATURE RESERVE** with a **10 m-** (33ft-) **DEEP LAGOON** fed by **UNDERGROUND CAVERNS** in the centre.

The world's **EIGHTH-LARGEST** island, Canada's **Victoria Island,** has a **LAKE ON IT** with an **ISLAND IN IT** that has a **LAKE ON IT** that itself has a **300 m-** (1,000ft-) **LONG ISLAND!**

There are up to **10,000 ISLANDS** and **ISLETS** in the **MEDITERRANEAN SEA.**

Fabulous
WATERFALLS

Waterfalls occur anywhere that a stream of water steeply drops down as it flows. They are usually formed when rivers erode softer rocks faster than harder rocks, leaving an overhang.

Known as the **"LAND OF A THOUSAND WATERFALLS"**, **NORWAY** has the most of any country, including all **10 of EUROPE'S HIGHEST.**

South America's **IGUAZÚ FALLS** is shaped like a **HORSESHOE** and stretches **2.7km** (1.7 miles), making it almost **3 times WIDER** than **NIAGARA FALLS.**

The multi-tiered **REICHENBACH FALLS** flows over **7 steps** as it cascades down from a glacier in the **SWISS ALPS.**

The **HIGHEST** waterfall on any continent is **VENEZUELA'S ANGEL FALLS,** with a drop of **979m** (3,212ft), making it nearly **3 TIMES** the height of the **EIFFEL TOWER.**

Iguazú Falls is made up of **275** individual **CASCADING WATERFALLS.**

12,000-YEAR-OLD

NIAGARA FALLS is divided into **2 PARTS**. The **CANADIAN HORSESHOE FALLS** stands at **48 m** (162ft) high and the **AMERICAN FALLS** at **51 m** (167ft) high.

In **2009**, Tyler Bradt paddled over **PALOUSE FALLS** in Washington, USA, to set the record for the **HIGHEST WATERFALL PLUNGE** in a kayak, reaching around **160 KPH** (100mph) as he dropped **57.6 m** (189ft).

NIAGRA FALLS is slowly **ERODING AWAY**. At the current rate of erosion, it will have **DISAPPEARED** around **50,000 YEARS FROM NOW**.

The **WORLD'S LARGEST WATERFALL** is **3 KM** (1.8 miles) high! It is found **UNDERWATER** in a strait between Iceland and Greenland where **COLDER, DENSER WATER** falls below **WARMER WATER** over a **DROP IN THE OCEAN FLOOR**.

At **10.8 KM** (6.7 miles) across, **KHONE FALLS** in **LAOS** is one of the **WIDEST WATERFALLS** in the world.

The **FANG** in Colorado, USA, is a **FROZEN WATERFALL** in winter, when it forms a single **PILLAR OF ICE** that stands over **30 m** (100ft) tall.

Inga Falls on the **CONGO RIVER** only has a slight drop, but it has the **HIGHEST FLOW RATE** of any waterfall. **25,060 CUBIC M** (885,000 cubic ft) of **WATER** passes over its rapids **EVERY SECOND**.

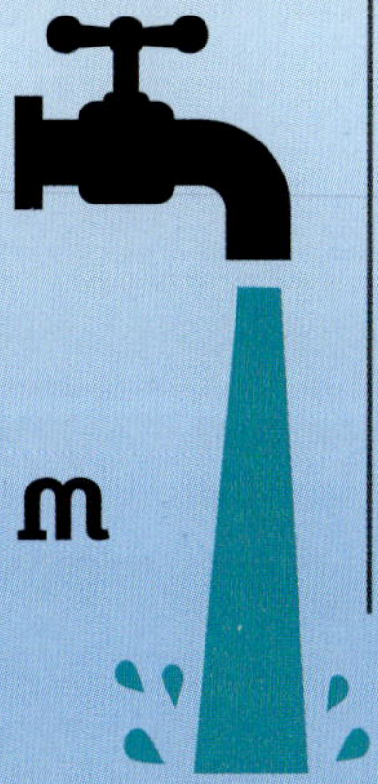

For part of February, **5 TO 15 MINUTES** before **SUNSET**, **HORSETAIL FALL** in Yosemite National Park, USA, looks like a **"firefall"** as the sunlight gives it an **ORANGEY GLOW**.

VICTORIA FALLS

Known by the local Lozi people as Mosi-oa-Tunya (Thundering Smoke), Victoria Falls is one of the world's largest waterfalls. Found along Africa's Zambezi River, the falls dramatically plunge into a deep chasm that leads to a series of epic gorges.

Victoria Falls straddles the **BORDER** between **2 countries, ZAMBIA** and **ZIMBABWE.**

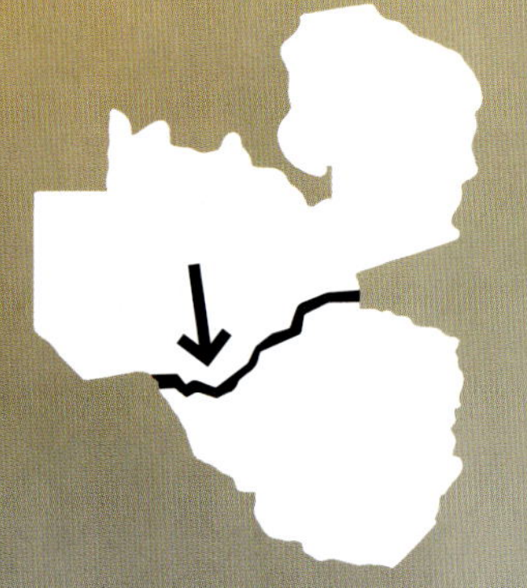

Water probably started flowing at this site around **5 MILLION YEARS AGO,** but the current falls are at most **250,000 years old.**

The **GIANT FRACTURE** in the rock that the falls flow over was opened about **110 MILLION years ago** through the splitting up of the **SUPERCONTINENT Gondwana.**

At **1,708 m** (5,603ft) **WIDE,** this is the world's **LARGEST** uninterrupted **curtain of falling water.**

The **Victoria Falls Bridge** is **200 m** (657ft) long and carries trains, cars, and people **128 m** (420ft) above the water.

THE ZAMBEZI flows along a flat **PLATEAU** before making a **SHEER DROP** of **108 m** (355ft) into a fracture in the rock.

There are **8 DEEP GORGES** stretching **150 km** (93 miles) after the falls that have been **SCULPTED** by the fast-moving water.

STONE ARTEFACTS discovered near the falls suggest **EARLY HUMANS** lived there **2 million years ago.**

The falls **FLOW** at an average rate of **1,100 CUBIC m** (39,000 cubic ft) **PER SECOND** – but its maximum recorded flow rate is nearly **10 TIMES** that!

DEVIL'S POOL, a natural, 3m- (10ft-) DEEP swimming hole on the EDGE OF THE FALLS, is accessible by BOAT during the DRY SEASON.

Victoria Falls is around 2 TIMES WIDER and 2 TIMES HIGHER than Niagara Falls.

Victoria Falls emits a rainbow-like mist that can be seen over 20KM (12 miles) away.

The SOUND of the falls can be heard up to 40KM (25 miles) away.

The BEDROCK of the falls is a "geological island" of BASALT that formed around 180 MILLION YEARS AGO from 1 MILLION YEARS of ERUPTIONS.

The **world's largest glacier** is SELLER GLACIER in ANTARCTICA. At **7,018 SQ KM** (2,710 sq miles), it is nearly the size of the GREEK ISLAND of CRETE.

If all of the **GLACIERS** and **ICE SHEETS** on Earth were to **MELT**, the **SEA LEVEL** would **RISE** around **70 m** (230ft), **FLOODING** every **COASTAL CITY** on the planet.

Around **91%** of all glacier ice on Earth is found in **Antarctica.**

SNOW is **90% AIR.** The process of it being **COMPACTED** into **glacier ice,** with only **20% AIR,** takes about **100 YEARS.**

GLACIER ICE is classed as a **MONO-MINERALIC** rock, made of just **1 MINERAL,** the crystalline form of H_2O (water).

GLACIAL ICE covers roughly **10%** of Earth's land area or around **15 MILLION SQ KM** (5.8 million sq miles).

Some tiny creatures live in glacier ice, including **MICROORGANISMS** and **INSECTS,** as well as **ICE WORMS** that can grow up to **2.5 cm** (1 in) long.

GLACIERS

A glacier is a large buildup of compacted snow with rocks and soil mixed in. They form over tens to hundreds of years in places with lots of snowfall where the average temperature stays around freezing. Glaciers move due to pressure from their own weight, sculpting the landscape around them as they flow and melt.

A **SINGLE ICE CRYSTAL** in a glacier can be up to **15cm** (6in) **ACROSS**, the size of an **apple**.

The **OLDEST** glacier ice on the planet, found in **ANTARCTICA**, is **4.6 million YEARS OLD.**

Alaska's **TAKU GLACIER** is one of the **THICKEST**, with a depth of up to **1,480m** (4,860ft).

Jakobshavn Isbræ glacier in **GREENLAND** is the world's **FASTEST-MOVING** glacier, **TRAVELLING** as much as **46m** (151ft) – the length of **2 TENNIS COURTS** – per day.

There are **GLACIERS** in **47 COUNTRIES** around the world, on every continent except **AUSTRALIA.**

Around **70%** of **EARTH'S FRESH WATER** is frozen in **GLACIER ICE.**

To be **CLASSIFIED** as an **ICEBERG**, the ice must rise at least

5m (16ft)

above the surface and be **29—50m** (98–164ft) thick.

Chunks of **FLOATING ICE** that rise **LESS THAN**

5m (16ft)

above sea level are called **bergy bits,** and chunks **UNDER**

1m (3ft) are called **growlers.**

An **ICEBERG** can be as tall as a

55- STOREY

building from top to bottom.

ICEBERGS release nutrients, such as **IRON**, as they melt. Giant icebergs can **FERTILIZE** an **AREA OF PLANKTON** all around them, with a diameter up to

10 times THEIR LENGTH.

Only around **10%** of an **ICEBERG** is visible.

90% of it is **UNDERWATER.**

ICEBERGS float because they are slightly **LESS DENSE** than **SEAWATER** – about

0.09 G/ML

(12oz/gallon) less dense.

ICEBERGS generally last **3—6 YEARS,** from the time they "CALVE" off glaciers to when they **COMPLETELY** melt away.

ICEBERGS

These large masses of ice break away from glaciers or ice shelves in polar regions and float away in the Arctic, North Atlantic, and Southern Oceans. They are made mostly of fresh water mixed with rock and dust. As they melt, they act like a river flowing into the sea, helping to rebalance its salt levels.

One of the **LARGEST-KNOWN** icebergs, called the **A23A,** was **4,000 SQ KM** (1,500 sq miles) – double the size of **GREATER LONDON!**

A23A formed in **1986,** making it the **OLDEST-KNOWN** iceberg. It weighs nearly **1 TRILLION TONNES.**

The **ICEBERG** that sunk the **269m–** (883ft-) long **TITANIC** likely reached **15–17m** (50–60ft) out of the water.

Around **10,000–15,000 ICEBERGS** calve from the **ANTARCTIC ICE SHEET** every year, losing **0.01%** of its mass.

Greenland's ice sheet calves around **30 MILLION TONNES** of icebergs every **HOUR.**

Over **1,000 ICEBERGS** float through an area known as **ICEBERG ALLEY** off **NEWFOUNDLAND, CANADA,** between May and June each year.

An average of **2.3 SHIPS** collide with **ICEBERGS** in the **NORTHERN HEMISPHERE** each year.

CHANGING PLANET

WEATHER & CLIMATE

For most places on Earth, weather is changeable. Sunshine, storms, and everything in between are caused by differences in temperature, pressure, moisture, cloudiness, and wind within masses of air. Climate is a location's weather conditions over a long period.

The **LOWEST** and **HIGHEST TEMPERATURES** recorded on Earth are

146°C

(262°F) apart.

Jet streams can blow at

442 KPH

(275mph).

The **SUNNIEST** place on Earth is a plateau in **CHILE'S**

Atacama Desert.

The radiation there has reached

2,177

WATTS PER SQ M (23,433 watts/sq ft), similar to the **SOLAR ENERGY** reaching

Venus!

The **BIGGEST TEMPERATURE SWING** in a single day was

57.2°C (103°F),

recorded in **MONTANA, USA,** in **January 1972.**

LARGE raindrops fall **FASTER** than **SMALL** ones, which can take up to

7 minutes

to reach the ground.

Both **fog** and **mist** are caused by **TINY** but **VISIBLE WATER PARTICLES** in the air, but fog reduces visibility more – to

1 km

(⅝ mile) or less.

The average **ROOF** would have

750 LITRES

(165 gallons) of water fall on it during just

1 cm

(⅓in) of **RAIN.**

Yakutsk, Siberia,

is the world's **COLDEST CITY,** with an average annual temperature of

–7.5°C

(18.5°F).

A **squall** happens when wind speeds up by at least **30 KPH** (18mph), blowing at **41 KPH** (25mph) or more for at least **1 minute.**

The **HIGHEST WIND SPEED** ever recorded on Earth was a gust on Australia's Barrow Island that reached **408 KPH** (253mph) – **FASTER** than a **RACING CAR.**

Weather systems are **MOVED AROUND** by bands of wind called **JET STREAMS, 6—13 KM** (4–8 miles) above Earth.

EVERY MINUTE, 1 billion tonnes of water falls to Earth as **PRECIPITATION.**

Around **98%** of **SEASONAL SNOW COVER** is in the Northern Hemisphere.

The **LARGEST HAIL** on record fell on **Bangladesh** in **APRIL 1986.** The hailstones weighed up to **1.02 KG** (2lb 4oz).

The **RAINIEST** place in the world is **MAWSYNRAM, INDIA,** which gets **1,197 cm** (471in) of rain **PER YEAR** – around **12 times** the global average.

Essential ATMOSPHERE

The gases that surround Earth are known as its atmosphere. They're kept close to the planet's surface by gravity. The atmosphere acts like a protective bubble, letting in the Sun's warm rays while shielding us from harmful radiation. It also includes the oxygen we breathe, so we couldn't live without it!

2 GASES make up about **99%** of Earth's atmosphere – it's **78% NITROGEN** and **21% OXYGEN.**

EXOSPHERE

THERMOSPHERE

MESOSPHERE

STRATOSPHERE

TROPOSPHERE

Earth has had **2 DIFFERENT ATMOSPHERES** before the current one – the **ORIGINAL ATMOSPHERE** **4.5 billion** years ago was probably mainly **HYDROGEN** and **HELIUM.**

There are **5 MAIN LAYERS** in the **ATMOSPHERE** between Earth's surface and outer space, from the **TROPOSPHERE** to the **EXOSPHERE.**

The **WEIGHT** of the **ATMOSPHERE** is similar to that of a **10m** (33ft) layer of **WATER COVERING** the planet, but it is **SPREAD OUT,** so we don't notice it.

More than **2 BILLION YEARS AGO,** many species of **microbe** went **EXTINCT** because the **OXYGEN** in the new atmosphere was **TOXIC** to them.

Around **75%** of the **ATMOSPHERE'S MASS** is contained in the **TROPOSPHERE** — the layer **CLOSEST TO EARTH.**

The **TROPOSPHERE VARIES IN HEIGHT.** It's up to **20 km** (12 miles) at the **EQUATOR** and only about **6 km** (4 miles) at the **POLES.**

99% of all the **WATER VAPOUR** in the atmosphere is in the **TROPOSPHERE,** so most **CLOUDS** are found here.

OZONE, a molecule with **3 atoms** of **OXYGEN,** is concentrated in the **SECOND LAYER,** the **STRATOSPHERE.** It shields the Earth from **HARMFUL ULTRAVIOLET LIGHT.**

Humans could not survive without a **PRESSURIZED SUIT** at **18,000 m** (60,000 ft) or higher in the atmosphere, as the **AIR PRESSURE** that far above Earth is so low that **BLOOD** would **BOIL** at normal body temperature.

The **coldest** temperatures in the atmosphere are found in the **THIRD LAYER,** the **MESOSPHERE.** They can drop to **−90°C** (−130°F).

The **FOURTH LAYER,** the **THERMOSPHERE,** is the **HOTTEST** one, because of **solar radiation,** with temperatures up to **2,000°C** (3,630°F).

Most **SCIENTISTS** believe the atmosphere's **fifth layer,** the **EXOSPHERE,** ends about **10,000 KM** (6,215 miles) above Earth's surface.

ATMOSPHERIC BROWN CLOUDS, formed by **AIR POLLUTANTS,** can reach heights of **3,000 m** (9,850 ft) – almost **8 TIMES** the height of the **EMPIRE STATE BUILDING.**

Cyclical
SEASONS

Earth has seasons because it spins at an angle relative to its orbit around the Sun. Different regions around the globe experience different seasons based on their locations. While mid-latitude countries have spring, summer, autumn, and winter, tropical countries may have just two seasons, one wet and one dry.

EARTH'S TILT varies from **22.1°** to **24.5°** over a **40,000-YEAR CYCLE.** The **GREATER** its **TILT,** the more **EXTREME** the planet's seasons are.

CLIMATE CHANGE is expanding the **TROPICAL CLIMATE ZONE** by over **0.1 degrees** of latitude every **10 YEARS,** so more places are getting **2 SEASONS** instead of **4.**

2024 was the **HOTTEST SUMMER** in the **NORTHERN HEMISPHERE** for **2,000 years.**

In **Sweden** and **Finland, SPRING** officially begins when the **DAILY AVERAGE TEMPERATURE** stays above **0°C** (32°F).

Some **CALENDARS** in **South Asia,** such as the **HINDU** and **TAMIL** calendars, list **6 SEASONS.**

Each **equinox** and **solstice** takes place **6 hours** later every year between **LEAP YEARS.**

METEOROLOGISTS (weather experts) divide the seasons into **3 CALENDAR MONTHS** each. In the Northern Hemisphere, **SPRING** starts on **1 MARCH,** and so on.

The **MONSOON SEASON** in the **INDIAN SUBCONTINENT** can bring **1.5 m** (5ft) of **SUMMER RAINFALL.**

Around **20%** of **BIRD SPECIES** **migrate** in **AUTUMN.**

M T W T F S S

Because Earth's orbit around the Sun is **OVAL-SHAPED,** astronomical **SPRING–SUMMER** in the **NORTHERN HEMISPHERE** is longer than **AUTUMN–WINTER** by **7 days.**

Parts of **FINLAND** see about **18.5 hours** of **DAYLIGHT** in **MID-JUNE** and less than **6 hours** in **DECEMBER.**

People living around the **EQUATOR** experience about **12 hours** of **DAYLIGHT** and **12 hours** of **DARKNESS** all year round.

Due to Earth's **ELLIPTICAL ORBIT,** the Northern Hemisphere is **5 million** KM (3.1 million miles) closer to the Sun in winter than it is at **MIDSUMMER.**

In the **NORTHERN HEMISPHERE,** the **WINTER SOLSTICE** falls on the **SHORTEST** day of the year – **21 or 22 December.** In the **SOUTHERN HEMISPHERE,** this is the **LONGEST DAY,** when the **SUMMER SOLSTICE** takes place.

SUMMER brings constant sunlight to the **POLES.** In the northernmost inhabited place in Europe, the Sun **DOES NOT SET** for **4 months** from April to August. This is called the **MIDNIGHT SUN.**

As the Earth takes **365.26** **DAYS** to orbit the Sun, a **CALENDAR DAY** is added every **4 years** (a **LEAP YEAR**) to keep the seasons consistent.

Earth has had at least **5 MAJOR ICE AGES.**

850—630 MILLION YEARS AGO, in the **CRYOGENIAN ICE AGE,** ice covered all or most of the planet, creating a **"snowball Earth".**

The **LATEST INTERGLACIAL** began about **11,700 YEARS AGO.**

The most recent time when **GLACIERS** reached their **PEAK** was around **26,000** to **19,000 YEARS AGO:** the **LAST GLACIAL MAXIMUM (LGM).**

The **HURONIAN ICE AGE** was the **LONGEST:** it started **2.4 billion YEARS AGO** and **LASTED 300 MILLION YEARS.**

During the **LGM, GLACIERS** covered about **25%** of Earth's land, compared to **10% TODAY.**

In the **LGM,** the average **GLOBAL TEMPERATURE** was about **6°C** (11°F) **COLDER THAN TODAY.**

During the **LAST GLACIAL MAXIMUM,** the **sea level** in **EUROPE** was about **120 m** (about 400ft) **LOWER** than now.

Ice-age animals had **SPECIAL ADAPTATIONS** for surviving freezing conditions. **WOOLLY MAMMOTHS** had up to **8cm** (3in) of **FAT** under their skin and **HAIR** up to **50cm** (20in) long.

ICE AGES

An ice age is a period when thick ice sheets cover large areas of Earth's surface. They take place in long cycles that correspond to changes in our planet's tilt and orbit. Within an ice age, there are colder periods called glacials, when glaciers are advancing. Warmer periods, when glaciers are retreating, are called interglacials.

There are shorter **COOLER** and **WARMER** periods between glacials, called **STADIALS** and **INTERSTADIALS**. A stadial known as **THE LITTLE ICE AGE** occurred from **1550 to 1850,** greatly affecting the **NORTHERN HEMISPHERE'S CLIMATE.**

The **FIRST MOSSLIKE PLANTS,** appearing around **470 million YEARS AGO,** may have **TRIGGERED AN ICE AGE** by sucking **CARBON DIOXIDE** from the **ATMOSPHERE.**

According to geologists, **WE ARE STILL LIVING IN AN ICE AGE,** the **QUATERNARY GLACIATION** that began around **2.6 million** years ago.

Around **12,000–10,000 YEARS AGO,** most of the **LARGEST MAMMALS,** known as **megafauna,** that lived during the last glacial became **EXTINCT.**

Around **8,000 YEARS** ago, Earth **THAWED** rapidly. The Antarctic ice sheet **THINNED** by **450m** (1,500ft) in under **200 YEARS.**

HUMAN ACTIVITIES have caused the Earth to **WARM 10 times faster** than at the **END OF AN ICE AGE.**

Sky-high
CLOUDS

Clouds are masses of tiny water droplets or ice particles that condense around seed particles, such as dust, salt, or soot, as the air cools. There are over a hundred kinds, classified according to their shape and height in the sky.

An amateur **METEOROLOGIST** in England defined **4 CLOUD TYPES** in **1803** that are the basis for today's classifications: **cumulus, stratus, cirrus, and nimbus.**

CHUUK LAGOON, a coral island in the **CENTRAL PACIFIC,** is the **cloudiest place** in the world, with an average of **92.3%** cloud cover.

CLOUDS generally appear **white** because the water in them **SCATTERS** all **7 COLOURS** found in **WHITE LIGHT** equally.

CLOUDS are also classed by **HEIGHT: LOW** is **BELOW 2,000m** (7,000ft), **HIGH** is **ABOVE 5,000m** (17,000ft), and **MEDIUM** is **IN BETWEEN** those two.

The average **WATER DROPLET** in a cloud is **1 million TIMES SMALLER** than a **RAINDROP.**

The **DROPLETS** are so tiny, they can **REMAIN LIQUID** at temperatures of up to **−30°C** (-22°F).

The **MICROSCOPIC WATER DROPLETS** in clouds are only **0.005−0.05mm** (0.0002–0.002in) across.

Many **CLOUDS** last only **15 minutes,** but **STORM CLOUDS** can linger for **HOURS** or even **WEEKS.**

Clouds are mostly **MADE OF AIR,** but they carry an average of **5G** of **WATER PER CUBIC M** (0.005oz per cubic ft).

An average **CUMULONIMBUS** storm cloud weighs about **400 TONNES –** as much as **2 BLUE WHALES.**

Multi-level **CUMULONIMBUS** clouds are the **TALLEST** type of cloud, averaging around **12 KM** (40,000ft) from bottom to top.

There are **4 "SPECIES"** of fluffy **CUMULUS** clouds. Their bases all begin at heights of **365–2,000M** (1,200–6,500ft).

NASA'S EARTH OBSERVATORY estimates that around **67%** of **EARTH'S SURFACE** is **COVERED BY CLOUD** at any time.

ONLY VISIBLE when light strikes them at **CERTAIN ANGLES** from below, wispy **noctílucent** ("NIGHT-SHINING") clouds are easiest to see **40 mínutes** after **SUNSET.**

NOCTILUCENT clouds are the **HIGHEST** in the sky, forming around **80 KM** (50 miles) above Earth – that's **7 TIMES** as **HIGH** as commercial **AEROPLANES** usually fly.

A **2024** study showed that the **HUNDREDS OF TONNES** of **WATER VAPOUR** that **ROCKETS** release as they launch increase **CLOUD FORMATION.**

Terrible
TORNADOES

Tornadoes are powerful spinning winds that build up at the top of a storm cloud. As warm air rises and begins turning, it forms a funnel shape. Cold air currents push the funnel downwards. When it touches the ground, it becomes a tornado – a towering storm powerful enough to rip up trees and houses in its path.

The **WINDS** in a tornado can **SPIN** at speeds up to **480 KPH** (300mph), much faster than an **F1 RACING CAR.**

"**Tornado Alley**", which runs across the USA from **TEXAS** in the south up to **SOUTH DAKOTA**, sees around **1,000** tornadoes every year.

In **APRIL 2011,** **758** tornadoes were recorded in the US, the **MOST** ever for a month.

The **DEADLIEST** tornado struck **Bangladesh** in **1989** when an estimated **1,300** people were killed.

During a huge tornado **OUTBREAK** in 2011, **207** separate tornadoes were recorded in the Midwest USA over one **24-HOUR PERIOD.**

The US averages **1,200** tornadoes a year while the **REST OF THE WORLD** averages **200—300.**

ARGENTINA has the **MOST TORNADOES** of anywhere in the Southern Hemisphere, around **7 ANNUALLY.**

One tornado recorded by **RADAR** in **OKLAHOMA, USA,** in **2013** had a diameter of **4.2 KM** (2.6 miles).

Tornadoes are **MEASURED** using the **FUJITA SCALE** (F-scale) from the **weakest, F0,** to the **strongest, F5,** with a windspeed over **320 KPH** (200mph).

In **1931**, a tornado in **MISSISSIPPI, USA,** lifted a **75-tonne train** **24 m** (80ft) from its track along with **117 PASSENGERS.**

In the **NORTHERN HEMISPHERE,** about **98%** of tornadoes spin in an **ANTICLOCKWISE DIRECTION.**

A tornado that hit **MISSOURI, USA,** in **MAY 2011** caused **£1.7 billion** in damage.

Tornadoes can last for **SECONDS OR HOURS.** The longest recorded lasted **3.5 hours.**

In **1925**, one tornado crossed **3 US states (MISSOURI, ILLINOIS, AND INDIANA)** on its **352 KM-** (218 mile-) long route.

England is hit by **MORE TORNADOES** than any other country for its area, an average **2.2 per 10,000 SQ KM** (3,861 sq miles) each year, though **FEW ARE SERIOUS.**

In May 2007, **123 tornadoes** broke out in **4 US STATES** over **3 days.**

Lightning is
5 times
HOTTER than the
**SURFACE OF
THE SUN.**

Each lightning strike produces
around **2 KG** (4lb 6oz) of
NITROGEN OXIDES, which react
with **OXYGEN** to add to the protective
layer of **OZONE** in our atmosphere.

Land in the **TROPICS**
gets around
70%
of Earth's lightning
each year while the
ARCTIC and **ANTARCTIC**
get practically none.

HEAT LIGHTNING is light
reflected in the sky from distant
ELECTRICAL STORMS up to
160 KM
(100 miles) **AWAY —**
too far to see the bolts or hear
the accompanying thunder.

BOLTS OF LIGHTNING are generally **2 – 3 cm** (around 1 in) thick.

Thunder, the sonic boom caused by
lightning, can be **HEARD** up to around
16 KM
(10 miles) **AWAY**
from a lightning strike.

SOUND travels at
343 METRES PER SECOND
(1,125 ft per second).
So, if you see a bolt of lightning strike
1 KM (⅗ mile) **AWAY,**
you will hear the thunder
around **3 SECONDS LATER.**

Thunderclaps
are around
120
DECIBELS –
32 TIMES louder
than a **VACUUM
CLEANER.**

Lightning does not travel at the
SPEED OF LIGHT (1,079 million kph /
670 million mph). It goes a much slower
435,000 KPH
(270,000 mph).

LIGHTNING

As warm air lifts icy particles to the top of storm clouds, the particles knock together, building up static electrical charges. When the difference in positive and negative charges becomes too great within the cloud or between the cloud and ground, they discharge as a powerful electrical current in a flash of lightning.

A single **THUNDERCLOUD** has around

2 BILLION

WATTS OF POWER, more than the most powerful **NUCLEAR PLANT.**

A stroke of lightning has so much **ENERGY,** it can **HEAT UP** the surrounding **AIR** to

33,000°C (60,000°F).

EVERY SECOND, an average of

100

BOLTS of lightning **HIT EARTH.**

What are the chances you'll be **STRUCK BY LIGHTNING** any given year? Around

1 IN 1.2 MILLION.

Park ranger Roy Cleveland Sullivan was **STRUCK BY LIGHTNING**

7 times

and lived to tell the tales.

Around

24,000

PEOPLE DIE from lightning strikes each year, but about

90%

of those struck **SURVIVE.**

CATATUMBO LIGHTNING

Known as the lightning capital of the world, the point where Venezuela's Catatumbo River flows into Lake Maracaibo is home to an astonishing spectacle. Warm air from the Caribbean Sea meets cold storm clouds from the surrounding mountains, making for a "never-ending" electrical storm. Catatumbo is a Barí name, meaning "House of Thunder", and it rumbles there for hours a day throughout the rainy season.

LAKE MARACAIBO is a
13,280-SQ-KM
(5,130-sq-mile) inlet of the **CARIBBEAN SEA.**

A bank of **STORM CLOUDS** generally hovers
1 KM
(0.6 mile) above the lake.

The **RIVER BASIN** is surrounded by
3 mountain ranges:
the **ANDES, PERIJÁ MOUNTAINS,** and **MÉRIDA'S CORDILLERA.**

The **CATATUMBO RIVER** flows into **LAKE MARACAIBO** from its headwaters
338 KM
(210 miles) away in northern **COLOMBIA.**

The storm rages up to
10
HOURS PER DAY.

A massive **ELECTRICAL** storm hits **CATATUMBO** up to **160 NIGHTS** every year.

The **BEST TIME** to see it is in the **tenth month** of the year and height of the **RAINY SEASON,** OCTOBER.

Catatumbo records around **1.2 MILLION** lightning strikes per year.

CATATUMBO holds the record for the **HIGHEST CONCENTRATION** of lightning, with

250

STRIKES
PER SQ KM
(⅖ sq mile)
ANNUALLY.

The next highest concentration is

158

STRIKES
PER SQ KM
(⅖ sq mile), in a village in the **DEMOCRATIC REPUBLIC OF THE CONGO.**

The storms produce up to

280

LIGHTNING STRIKES
per hour, with

16 to 40

FLASHES A MINUTE.

There were **ZERO LIGHTNING STRIKES** at **CATATUMBO** between **JANUARY** and **MARCH 2010** due to a drought.

10

MINUTES
of Catatumbo lightning produces enough **ELECTRICITY** to light up **EVERY LIGHT BULB** in **SOUTH AMERICA.**

You can **SEE** the lightning at **CATATUMBO** from up to

400 KM

(250 miles) away, and the thunder can be **HEARD** from up to

24 KM

(15 miles) away.

It **DOES NOT** need to be freezing for it to **SNOW**. If the **AIR TEMPERATURE** is

2°C (35.6°F),
PRECIPITATION will fall as **SNOW**.

There are more than

6,000
SKI RESORTS for snow sports worldwide. **EUROPE** has the **MOST** of any continent with **3,945**.

Snow is **LESS LIKELY** to fall at temperatures **BELOW**

−9°C
(15°F) because **VERY COLD AIR** tends to hold **LESS MOISTURE**.

SNOWFLAKES are so light that they generally **FALL** for about

1 hour
before they reach the **GROUND**.

SNOW is great at **INSULATING** because it's over **90% trapped air. IGLOOS** reach temperatures of

15°C (59°F)
even when it's as cold as

−45°C
(−49°F) outside.

SNOWFLAKES form from

6-SIDED
ICE CRYSTALS, and the temperature affects their shape. Each flake is **UNIQUE**.

Individual **SNOWFLAKE CRYSTALS** are **2−10 mm** (0.08−⅜ in) across.

EVERY YEAR, at least

1,000,000,000,000,000,000,000,000
(one septillion) **SNOWFLAKES** fall around the **WORLD**.

SNOWFLAKES form around

1 SINGLE
PARTICLE of **DUST, GRAIN** of **POLLEN,** or **BACTERIUM**.

Spectacular SNOW

Snow is an icy form of precipitation that forms as water vapour freezes, creating snow crystals that fall as downy flakes. If the ground temperature is around or below freezing, snow can accumulate into a dusting or high enough to cover whole buildings.

In **CANADA, 65%** of the land is **COVERED WITH SNOW** for at least **6 MONTHS** a year.

AVALANCHES can move **FASTER** than

320 KPH

(200mph).

The **DEADLIEST BLIZZARD** in history took place in **IRAN** in **1972**. It left people in **200 VILLAGES** trapped, **KILLING** over **4,000.**

Snow impacts **GLOBAL HEATING AND COOLING PATTERNS** as the ground **ABSORBS**

5 times

as much **HEAT** from the Sun when it is **NOT COVERED** with snow.

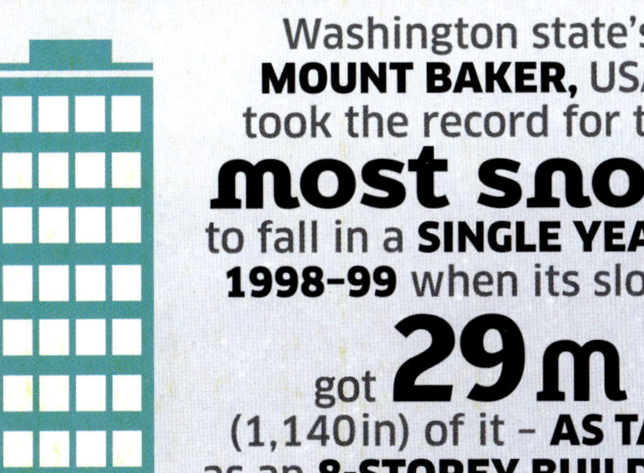

Washington state's **MOUNT BAKER**, USA, took the record for the **most snow** to fall in a **SINGLE YEAR** in **1998–99** when its slopes got **29 m** (1,140in) of it – **AS TALL** as an **8-STOREY BUILDING!**

The **JAPANESE ALPS** have one of the **DEEPEST ANNUAL SNOWFALL** averages, receiving around

17.6 m

(58ft) **A YEAR.**

Around **10%** of **EARTH'S SURFACE** is permanently **COVERED** in ice and snow. **SEASONAL SNOW** can cover up to **30%** of the land on Earth.

A tropical cyclone can be up to **2,000 KM** (more than 1,200 miles) **WIDE**, with an **"EYE"** (area of calm weather in the centre of the cyclone) up to **100KM** (60 miles) **ACROSS**.

THE PACIFIC OCEAN has the most tropical storms **(57%)**, followed by the **INDIAN OCEAN (31%)** and then the **ATLANTIC OCEAN (12%)**.

HURRICANES can be **PREDICTED** up to **5 days** **IN ADVANCE**, allowing people to move to **SAFETY**.

CYCLONES form when **OCEAN WATERS** become **EXTREMELY WARM** – at least **27°C** (80°F).

The **DEADLIEST** tropical storm ever recorded hit **Bangladesh** in 1970 – up to **500,000** people **DIED** because of the storm surge.

There are **5 CATEGORIES** of hurricanes – the **MOST POWERFUL** is **CATEGORY 5**, where the **WIND SPEED** reaches more than **252 KPH** (157mph).

Powerful tropical cyclones create **WINDS** of up to **240 KPH** (150mph), with **GUSTS** of more than **320 KPH** (200mph).

Tropical storms can cause **STORM SURGES**, where **OCEAN WAVES** up to **6 m** (20ft) high sweep over the coast.

CLIMATE CHANGE is making cyclones more intense and faster to develop. In **2023**, **HURRICANE IDALIA** went from a **Category 1** to **4** in **24 hours**.

If winds reach **63 KPH** (39mph), it is a **TROPICAL STORM** and it is given a name; at **116 KPH** (72mph), it's a **TROPICAL CYCLONE**.

The tropical cyclone that caused the most **EXPENSIVE** property **DAMAGE** in history was **Hurricane Katrina** in the **USA**, in 2005: **£93.3 billion.**

Tropical cyclones form in **THE TROPICS**, between approximately **5°** and **30°** latitude.

TROPICAL CYCLONES

These huge, destructive, rapidly rotating storms originate over the tropical oceans around the Equator. They go by different names depending on where they occur. They are called hurricanes over the North Atlantic and northeast Pacific, typhoons over the northwest Pacific, and cyclones over the South Pacific and Indian Oceans.

The **top 3** countries hit with the **MOST** tropical cyclones are all in **ASIA: CHINA, THE PHILIPPINES,** and **JAPAN.**

There are about **80** tropical storms **every year.**

Formidable
FLOODS

During a flood, land that is normally dry is covered by water. The most common cause of flooding is too much rain falling too quickly, which makes rivers overflow their banks. Storms and tsunamis can also cause coastal flooding. Floods can be useful, depositing nutrient-rich sediment for farming, but also destructive, threatening life and spreading hazardous waste.

Around **1.47 BILLION PEOPLE** (or **19%** of the **WORLD'S POPULATION**) face intense **FLOODING RISK.**

A **FLASH FLOOD** is one that occurs within **6 hours of rainfall,** but they can happen in as quickly as **1 MINUTE!**

MASS MELTING of glaciers has caused **megafloods** in the past. **THE ENGLISH CHANNEL** was likely created by a **LAKE OVERFLOWING** an **ICE WALL 450,000 YEARS AGO.**

The Netherlands, **1/3** of which is **BELOW SEA LEVEL,** is the country with the **HIGHEST FLOOD RISK.** Nearly **3** out of every **5 INHABITANTS** are under threat from flooding.

Around **60%** of floodplains in **Europe** are used for **FARMING.**

Since 1990, flooding has accounted for **42%** of **NATURAL DISASTERS,** making it the most common type of disaster.

THE CHANG JIANG (Yangtze River) **FLOOD** of **1931** in **CHINA** was likely the **DEADLIEST** in human history. An estimated **3.7 MILLION PEOPLE** lost their lives.

As little as **60 cm** (2ft) of moving water can **SWEEP A CAR AWAY.**

A person can be **KNOCKED DOWN** by just **15 cm** (6 in) of **RUSHING WATER.**

In **OHIO, USA,** in **1990, 10 cm** (4in) of **RAIN** that fell in **UNDER 2 HOURS** created a **9 m-** (30ft-) tall wall of water.

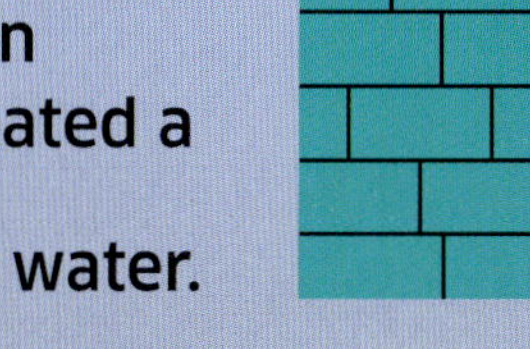

In some areas, flooding is up to **900% MORE LIKELY** today than it was **50 YEARS AGO.**

The size of **FLOODPLAIN AREAS** may increase by up to **45–55%** by the year **2100** due to rising sea levels and increasing storms and rainfall.

As land is **BUILT ON,** it becomes **LESS ABLE** to **ABSORB RAINFALL.** Runoff that leads to flooding is **2–6 TIMES MORE LIKELY** in **URBAN ENVIRONMENTS.**

TOP 10 HOTTEST COUNTRIES

BURKINA FASO • Africa • Average temperature: **29.3°C (84.7°F)**

1

It may not seem like 29.3°C (84.7°F) is too toasty until you consider that this is Burkina Faso's average mean air temperature (the average of all recorded temperatures added up over a year, including lows). Parts of the country can reach a sizzling 47°C (117°F) in summer.

2 **MALI** • Africa • Average temperature: **29.2°C (84.6°F)**
Like Burkina Faso and the next two countries on this list, Mali is cut across by Africa's Sahel, a semi-arid region on the southern border of the Sahara desert that often experiences bouts of extreme heat and drought.

3 **SENEGAL** • Africa • Average temperature: **28.9°C (84°F)**
Senegal is the westernmost country in Africa, with landscapes that range from desert to mangrove swamps. Its dry interior has recorded temperatures as high as 54°C (129.2°F), and it's projected to get even hotter due to human-driven climage change.

4 **MAURITANIA** • Africa • Average temperature: **28.8°C (83.9°F)**
Located entirely in the Sahara and Sahel, Mauritania is covered with dunes, arid plains, and plateaus. Its land is mostly desert, which has been expanding since the 1960s.

5 **TUVALU** • Oceania • Average temperature: **28.6°C (83.5°F)**
This series of coral islands in the South Pacific is hot all year round. It has a tropical climate, with dry and rainy seasons, but the amount of rainfall varies greatly from year to year.

6 **DJIBOUTI** • Africa • Average temperature: **28.5°C (83.3°F)**
Djibouti is in the Horn of Africa, along a strait that runs between the Red Sea and Gulf of Aden. It is at its hottest when dry, dusty winds blow across it from the desert.

7 **THE GAMBIA** • Africa • Average temperature: **28.4°C (83.1°F)**
Located in West Africa, the Gambia is the continent's smallest country. It is entirely surrounded by Senegal aside from its 80km (50-mile) coast on the Atlantic Ocean and has a long dry season.

8 **MALDIVES** • Asia • Average temperature: **28.1°C (82.6°F)**
This archipelago, stretching across the Equator in the Indian Ocean, is Asia's smallest country. It also has the lowest elevation of any in the world, which makes it constantly hot and humid and vulnerable to being submerged by rising sea levels.

9 **BENIN** • Africa • Average temperature: **28°C (82.4°F)**
A small tropical country in West Africa, Benin is famous for its lagoons and coconut palms. The south has four seasons, but the north has only two – dry and wet.

10 **PALAU** • Oceania • Average temperature: **27.9°C (82.2°F)**
Palau is an archipelago with more than 300 islands in the Micronesia region of the Pacific. It has a tropical climate and is wet all year round, with rainfall topping 350cm (140in) in some years.

Raging
WILDFIRES

Forest fires, wildfires, and bushfires are uncontrollable blazes that rip through woods and grassland. The fires can be triggered by lightning or by human activity. While some are part of the natural cycle, allowing new growth to sprout from ash-enriched soil, fires can cause enormous damage to forests and animals.

Plants with **UNDERGROUND STEM STRUCTURES** are the **"FIRST RETURNERS"**. Ferns can sprout up just **3 weeks** after a fire.

SOUTH AFRICA'S fire lily only **BLOOMS** after natural brush fires. The **SMOKE** triggers the appearance of **1—12** RED, TUBULAR, **6-PETALLED FLOWERS** on each stalk.

GIANT SEQUOIA trees have **fire-resistant bark** up to **60cm** (2ft) thick and need the **HEAT** of a fire to **RELEASE** their **SEEDS** from cones.

WILDFIRES can reach **TEMPERATURES** as **high** as **800°C** (1,470°F).

WILDFIRES can spread as **fast** as **23 KPH** (14mph).

More than **4 out of 5** WILDFIRES are started by **people.**

The **2019–2020 AUSTRALIAN BUSHFIRE SEASON** was the **WORST** in recent history, burning an estimated **186,000 SQ KM** (71,815 sq miles) and **DESTROYING 3,000** HOMES and **BUILDINGS.**

The Australian bushfires from **2019** to **2020** caused the **death** or **displacement** of an estimated **3 BILLION ANIMALS.**

FOREST FIRES are **RESPONSIBLE** for **33%** about of annual **TREE LOSS.**

An average **4,850 SQ KM** (1,875 sq miles) of **US WOODLAND** is burnt each year in around **60,000 wildfires.**

Forest fires generally last **3–6 WEEKS.** One of the **LONGEST,** in Canada in **1950,** lasted for **5 months.**

From **2023** to **2024,** wildfires added around **8.6 billion tonnes** of **CARBON DIOXIDE** to the **ATMOSPHERE.**

CALIFORNIA'S 2018 **"Camp Fire"** caused **£9.8 BILLION** of damage, one of the **DEADLIEST** and **COSTLIEST** wildfires ever.

Between **2001** and **2023,** the **AREA BURNED** by forest fires increased by **5.4%** every year.

RUSSIA has **LOST** an average of **250,000 SQ KM** (966,500 sq miles) of tree cover to wildfires **EVERY YEAR THIS CENTURY.**

GREENHOUSE GASES that trap heat, such as **CARBON DIOXIDE (CO₂)** and **METHANE**, are necessary for keeping our planet warm – without them, **EARTH** would average **–20°C** (-10°F).

Today, **HUMAN ACTIVITIES** are generating too much **GREENHOUSE GAS.** The concentration of CO₂ alone has **INCREASED** by **50%** since **PRE-INDUSTRIAL TIMES.**

The last time levels of **CARBON DIOXIDE (CO₂)** in the **ATMOSPHERE** were as high as today was **4.5 million** YEARS AGO.

FOSSIL FUELS, including **OIL, GAS,** and **COAL,** are the biggest causes of global warming. The use of them accounts for **3/4** of global greenhouse gas emissions.

METHANE is **80 times** more powerful than CO₂ at trapping heat, but CO₂ can **REMAIN** in the atmosphere for **HUNDREDS OF YEARS** longer.

CATTLE RAISED for **BEEF** release **105 BILLION KG** (231 billion lb) of **METHANE** each year.

Humans generate **60%** of **METHANE** emitted, and **37%** of it comes from **LIVESTOCK** and **AGRICULTURE.**

Destructive
CLIMATE CHANGE

Climate change is the gradual shift of temperature and weather patterns around the world. Some changes are part of a natural cycle while some are caused by human activities, such as industry, agriculture, and fossil fuel use. The effects of climate change include melting ice, rising sea levels, wildfires, storms, and drought, which can all put life at risk.

In **2015,** the governments of **196 COUNTRIES** agreed on targets to **LIMIT** the global temperature **RISE** to **NO MORE THAN** **1.5°C** (2.7°F).

2023 was the **HOTTEST YEAR** since records began in 1850, **1.2°C** (2.1°F) **WARMER** than the 20th-century average.

SEA LEVELS have **RISEN** by about **20cm** (8in) in the last **100 YEARS.**

Due to **GLOBAL WARMING,** the world's ice sheets and glaciers are losing **1.3 trillion TONNES** of ice **EVERY YEAR.**

If the **GREENLAND ICE SHEET** were to completely melt, **SEA LEVELS** **WOULD RISE** by **7m** (23ft).

Over **410 million PEOPLE** may be at risk from **COASTAL FLOODING** due to rising sea levels by 2100.

A **2024** study estimates that as many as **3–6 million SPECIES** are at risk of **EXTINCTION** in the next **50 YEARS** due to **CLIMATE CHANGE.**

To prevent **GLOBAL WARMING** beyond **1.5°C** (2.7°F), **CARBON EMISSIONS** need to drop by **7.6%** every year.

More than **30%** of the world's **ELECTRICITY** is now generated using renewable sources such as **WIND** and **SOLAR.**

7 countries (**ALBANIA, BHUTAN, ETHIOPIA, ICELAND, PARAGUAY, NEPAL,** and **THE DEMOCRATIC REPUBLIC OF THE CONGO**) are powered by nearly

100% **RENEWABLE ENERGY.**

LIVING PLANET

Treeless
TUNDRA

Tundras are treeless areas around the Arctic and Antarctic, one of the toughest environments for plants and animals to live. These cold, windy, and mostly dry places are covered with snow throughout much of the year. Yet they are a permanent home to reindeer, wolves, foxes, and marmots.

The **AVERAGE TEMPERATURE** in the **ARCTIC TUNDRA** is a chilly **–34 to 6°C** (-30 to 20˚F).

TUNDRAS are generally **DRY.** They may only see **5—25cm** (6–10in) of **RAIN** in a **YEAR.**

In the tundra there are **ZONES** of **PERMAFROST,** with **LAYERS** of **FROZEN SOIL** and **DEAD PLANTS** up to **450m** (1,476ft) **DEEP.**

For **2 months** in **SUMMER,** the Sun may **SHINE** over the tundra for **24 HOURS A DAY.**

TUNDRAS cover about **20%** of **EARTH'S LAND.**

Due to a **WARMING CLIMATE,** all but **30%** of the **SIBERIAN TUNDRA** may be lost by **2050.**

Tundra **WINDS** can **BLOW** up to **100 KPH** (60mph).

The **SMALLEST TREE IN THE WORLD** grows in the tundra. The **DWARF WILLOW** only reaches **6.4 cm** (2.5 in) in **HEIGHT.**

The tundra **SUMMER** *growing season* lasts for just **50 TO 60 DAYS.**

Many birds, including **WADING BIRDS, DUCKS,** and up to **5 million SNOW GEESE,** fly to the **EURASIAN TUNDRA** to breed in summer.

Despite **TOUGH WEATHER** conditions, about **1,700 DIFFERENT PLANTS** live in the tundra.

The **ARCTIC TERN** breeds in **SUMMER** in the **NORTH** then flies over **30,000 KM** (19,000 miles) for a **SECOND SUMMER** in the Antarctic.

REINDEER MIGRATE between the tundra and forest in **HERDS** of up to **1 million** and cover **5,000 KM** (3,000 miles) each year.

48 SPECIES of **LAND MAMMAL** are found on the **ARCTIC TUNDRA,** including bears, wolves, foxes, reindeer, and rodents.

The **NORTH AMERICAN TUNDRA** covers an area of around **5.3 million SQ KM** (2 million sq miles).

Evergreen
TAIGA

Also known as boreal forest, the taiga spreads just below the Arctic Circle, between the tundra and temperate forests further south. It is made up of coniferous evergreen trees and is home to animals such as the Siberian tiger, moose, bears, and lynx.

TAIGA covers around **17 million sq km** (6.6 million sq miles) of **EARTH'S LAND.**

The temperature in the **Siberian taiga** can drop to **–60°C** (-76 °F).

The **LARGEST TAIGA** in the world crosses **5,800km** (3,600 miles) of northern Russia from the **PACIFIC OCEAN** to the **URAL MOUNTAINS.**

The world's largest deer, **THE MOOSE,** is found in the **TAIGA.** Its antlers can grow to be over **1.5m** (5ft) **ACROSS.**

The **GROWING SEASON** in the taiga lasts **130 days.**

There are an estimated **750 trillion TREES** growing in the **TAIGA.**

The **TAIGA** receives **40–100 cm** (16–39 in) of precipitation **EVERY YEAR,** mostly as **SNOW.**

THE SCOTS PINE is a common taiga tree that can grow to be **700 YEARS OLD.**

In **SPRING** as many as **3 billion birds MIGRATE** to breed in the taiga.

Due to **COLDER** conditions, trees in the **NORTHERN TAIGA** grow **6–15 m** (20–50 ft) high compared to **15–30 m** (50–100 ft) in the south.

The **LARGEST PREDATOR** in the taiga is the **BROWN BEAR,** which can **RAISE** itself to a height of **2.8 m** (9 ft).

RUSSIA'S TAIGA is the **LARGEST FOREST** in the world at over **12 million SQ KM** (4.6 million sq miles) in area.

The **RUSSIAN TAIGA** was completely covered with **GLACIERS** during the last ice age (glacial), **12,000 years ago.**

About **3.7 million** people live in **CANADA'S TAIGA,** including **70%** of its Indigenous communities.

Temperate forests grow at **LATITUDES** between

25—50 DEGREES

in both the **NORTHERN** and **SOUTHERN HEMISPHERES.**

TEMPERATE FORESTS make up around

25%

of the planet's forested land.

Temperate forests have existed on Earth since about

65.5 MILLION YEARS AGO,

when global **TEMPERATURES BEGAN TO COOL.**

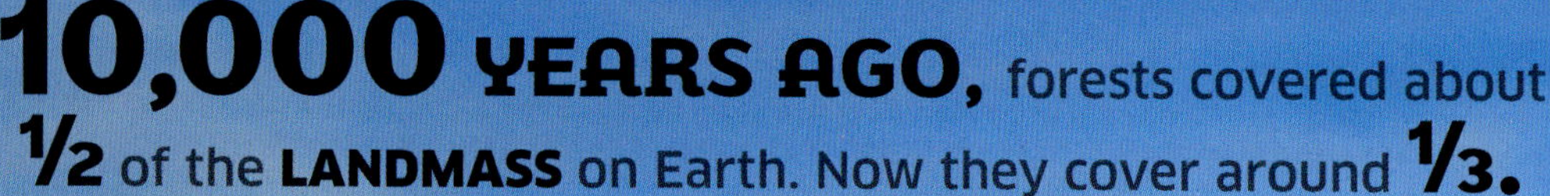

10,000 YEARS AGO, forests covered about ½ of the **LANDMASS** on Earth. Now they cover around ⅓.

DECIDUOUS LEAVES contain

3 pigments:

GREEN chlorophyll, **YELLOW** carotene, and **RED** anthocyanin. **AUTUMN COLOURS** come out when **COLD WEATHER DESTROYS** the **CHLOROPHYLL.**

A single **OAK TREE** produces up to

90,000 ACORNS in one year.

A **SINGLE TREE** absorbs

10—40 KG

(22-88lb) of **CARBON DIOXIDE** each year.

SCIENTISTS estimate there to be around **73,000 SPECIES OF TREE** on Earth.

Annually, **TEMPERATE FORESTS** receive between **75—150 cm** (30-60in) of **RAINFALL.**

TEMPERATE FOREST

These forests grow in regions with a temperate (moderate) climate. They can include deciduous trees, which lose their leaves, and evergreens. Temperate forests are found in every continent except Antarctica, providing a habitat for animals and timber for humans.

WOOD FUEL makes up **40%** of the **GLOBAL RENEWABLE ENERGY** supply. This is as much as **SOLAR, HYDROELECTRIC,** and **WIND POWER** combined.

At **68,000 SQ KM** (26,250 sq miles), **ALASKA'S TONGASS** is the **LARGEST TEMPERATE RAINFOREST** in the world.

The **LARGEST LIVING ORGANISM** is a **FOREST** of **47,000** **GENETICALLY IDENTICAL QUAKING ASPEN** trees that share a **ROOT SYSTEM.**

The **TALLEST TREE** in the world is in a **TEMPERATE REDWOOD FOREST** in **CALIFORNIA.** Called **Hyperion,** it is **116 m** (380.1 ft) **TALL.**

Biodiverse
RAINFORESTS

Rainforests are wet and leafy environments full of life, with trees growing tall to reach the sun. The tallest trees form a canopy, like an umbrella, blocking out sunlight. This is where most of the animals live. Tropical rainforests grow around the Equator, and temperate rainforests grow in cooler areas. Both get lots of rain!

RAINFORESTS get
200 to 1,000cm
(79–394in) of rain a year.
The **GLOBAL AVERAGE** is **100CM** (39in).

The **LARGEST TROPICAL RAINFOREST** in the world is the **AMAZON**, which covers
6.56
million sq km
(2.53 million sq miles) within **9 SOUTH AMERICAN COUNTRIES**.

Rainforests have
4 LAYERS
from **TOP** to **BOTTOM**: the **EMERGENT LAYER** (tops of the tallest trees), the **CANOPY**, the **UNDERSTORY**, and the **FOREST FLOOR**.

60%
of the Amazon rainforest is found in
Brazil.

It can take **10 MINUTES** for a **RAINDROP** to **FALL** from the canopy to the forest floor due to the dense vegetation.

Plants that grow on other plants and **GET WATER** from the **AIR** are called **EPIPHYTES.** Most of these, including **FERNS, MOSSES,** and **70%** of **ORCHIDS,** live in **RAINFOREST.**

An area equal to about **10 FOOTBALL FIELDS** of rainforest is being **FELLED** or **BURNED EVERY MINUTE** for logging, farming, or mining.

There may be **400 billion TREES GROWING** in the Amazon.

An estimated **50%** of all **PLANT** and **ANIMAL SPECIES** on Earth are found in tropical rainforests.

The **TALLEST** tropical rainforest trees are **KAPOKS,** which can grow **4 m** (13ft) a year to a height of **60 m** (200ft).

The **OLDEST** tropical rainforest is the **DAINTREE RAINFOREST** in northeastern **QUEENSLAND, AUSTRALIA,** which is thought to be **180 million years old.**

ONE LARGE Amazon rainforest tree can release **1,000 litres** (265 gallons) of water into the air in a day, enough to fill **10 BATHTUBS.**

Rainforests are found on all **6 INHABITED CONTINENTS.**

TEMPERATE RAINFOREST once covered up to **20%** of the **UK,** but it only covers **1%** today.

Less than **5%** of **SUNLIGHT** reaches the rainforest floor through all the **FOLIAGE.**

The **AMAZON** gets an average of **1.8 m** (6ft) to **3 m** (10ft) of **RAINFALL IN A YEAR.**

TOP 10 OLDEST TREES

PROMETHEUS • Bristlecone pine • USA
Age: **4,862+ YEARS**

1

When a gnarled pine like the one pictured was cut down in Nevada's Great Basin National Park in 1964, it turned out to have been the oldest-known living thing. It sprouted in 2900BCE, around when the Great Pyramids of Giza were built.

2 **METHUSELAH** • Bristlecone pine • USA • Age: **4,855**

Named after a Bible character who lived to be 969, Methuselah is actually five times older than that. Its exact location in the White Mountains of California is kept secret to protect it.

3 **GRAN ABUELO** • Patagonian cypress • Chile • Age: **3,653**

This towering conifer is found in the Alerce Costero Park in the Cordillera Pelada mountains of Chile. It is affectionately known as "Great-Grandfather", and one estimate suggests it could be more than 5,000 years old.

4 **GIANT SEQUOIA** • USA • Age: **3,266+**

Northern California has some of the biggest and oldest trees in the world. Four dead specimens from the Sierra Nevada mountains have been confirmed to have been more than 3,000 years old.

5 **THE SENATOR** • Bald cypress • USA • Age: **2,800**

This 50m-(165ft-) tall cypress towered over a Florida swamp until it was damaged by a 1925 hurricane and intentionally burnt down in 2012. Estimates of its age vary between 2,200 and 3,500 years old.

6 **SCOFIELD JUNIPER** • Sierra juniper • USA • Age: **2,675**

Another evergreen from California's Sierra Nevada range is known to have lived at least 2,675 years before its rings were counted in 1998.

7 **ROCKY MOUNTAIN BRISTLECONE PINE** • USA • Age: **2,466**

A relative of the older Great Basin bristlecones found on the West Coast of the USA, Rocky Mountain bristlecones in Colorado proved to be very old, too, based on samples.

8 **PANKE BAOBAB** • African baobab • Zimbabwe • Age: **2,419**

These trees are common to the savannas of sub-Saharan Africa. Radiocarbon dating of a dead tree in 2018 revealed it to have been the oldest-known flowering plant.

9 **JAYA SRI MAHA BODHI** • Sacred fig • Sri Lanka • Age: **2,310**

Planted by a Buddhist nun in 288BCE, this sacred fig is the oldest-known tree planted by a human. It is believed to be descended from the tree under which the Buddha was enlightened.

10 **QILIAN JUNIPER** • China • Age: **2,230**

Growing high up in the mountains of western China, this evergreen tree reaches heights of 20m (66ft) over hundreds of years.

Wild
WETLANDS

Any area of land that is regularly covered with water – all the time or seasonally – counts as a wetland. From swamps to marshes and lagoons to lakes, wetlands are the engines of the planet's biodiversity, and home to a fantastic array of plants and animals.

At **170,000 SQ KM** (65,600 sq miles), **BRAZIL'S PANTANAL** is the world's **LARGEST TROPICAL WETLAND.**

Around **80%** of The **PANTANAL** is flooded during the **RAINY SEASON.**

WETLANDS help keep **GLOBAL WARMING** at bay. **SALT MARSHES STORE CARBON** at **10 times** the rate of fully grown **TROPICAL FORESTS.**

WETLANDS provide natural protection against **FLOODING. 0.4 HECTARES** (1 acre) of wetland that is **30 cm** (1 ft) **DEEP** can **ABSORB** at least **1.25 million LITRES** (275,000 gallons) of **FLOODWATER.**

300–400 MILLION PEOPLE worldwide depend on and live near to **WETLANDS.**

40% of all the world's **ANIMALS** live or **BREED** in wetlands.

WETLAND AREAS cover roughly **6%** of Earth's **LAND SURFACE.**

The **PANTANAL** has the biggest **CROCODILIAN** population, with around **10 MILLION** CAIMANS.

Over the past **300 YEARS**, **85%** of wetlands have disappeared.

More than **75%** of **FISH HARVESTED COMMERCIALLY** around the world **DEPEND** on **WETLANDS.**

In the **UNITED STATES**, **1/3** of **ENDANGERED SPECIES** rely on wetlands for their **SURVIVAL.**

Each year **200 NEW SPECIES** are discovered in **FRESHWATER** wetlands.

SIBERIA'S GREAT VASYUGAN MIRE is the world's largest **PEAT BOG** and contains around **800,000 LAKES** and **POOLS.**

The winding waterways of the **KERALA BACKWATERS** in **INDIA** are made up of **LAGOONS** and **5 BIG CANALS** that are fed by **38 rivers.**

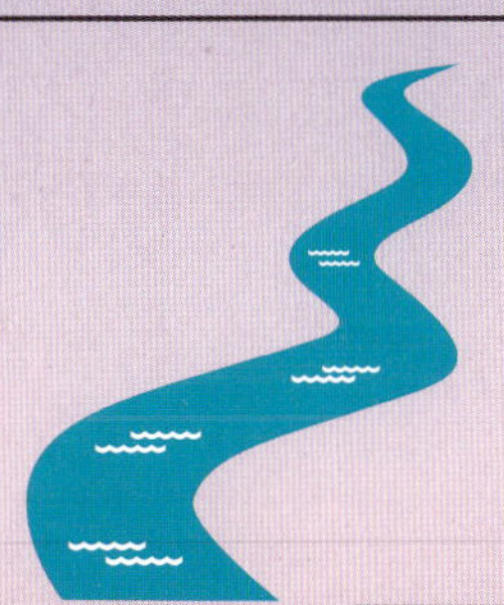

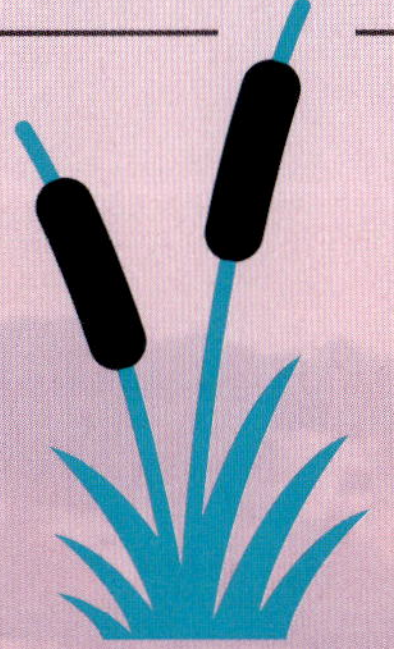

Many wetland **PLANTS** have **TALL STEMS.** **Bulrushes** can grow to **4 m** (12ft) **HIGH!**

WADING BIRDS flock to wetlands. **White ibises** gather in **"SUPERCOLONIES"** of more than **10,000** nesting birds in the **EVERGLADES** of Florida, USA.

Bone-dry
DESERTS

Deserts are found on every continent and cover around a fifth of Earth's land. They are vast areas that are extremely dry. People often think of deserts as super-hot places with lots of dunes, but some near the poles are very cold, and only around 20 per cent are covered with sand.

DESERTS receive less than **25 cm** (10 in) of **RAIN PER YEAR** – more than **75 cm** (29 in) **BELOW** the **GLOBAL AVERAGE.**

Chile's **ATACAMA** is the **DRIEST** hot desert. It receives **10–15 mm** (⅖–⅗ in) of **PRECIPITATION** (falling water) **PER YEAR** on average, mostly from **FOG.**

In the **DAY**, hot desert **TEMPERATURES** rise to an average of **38°C** (100.4°F); at **NIGHT**, they fall to an average of **−3.9°C** (25°F).

The **NAMIB** has some of Earth's **TALLEST** dunes, up to **383 m** (1,256 ft) high.

The **HOTTEST LAND SURFACE TEMPERATURE** ever recorded was a fiery **80.8°C** (177.4°F) in Iran's **LUT DESERT.**

The **LARGEST** desert is the **ANTARCTIC ICE SHEET,** measuring **13,960,000 SQ KM** (5,390,000 sq miles).

The massive **SAHARA** spans **4,800 KM** (3,000 miles) of **NORTH AFRICA,** covering an area **GREATER** than the **USA.**

DUNES MOVE slowly over time in the wind. The **FASTEST** can travel **70 m** (230 ft) per year.

The **WELWITSCHIA** of the **NAMIB DESERT** is one of the **LONGEST-LIVING** plants. It can **LIVE** for

1,000 YEARS.

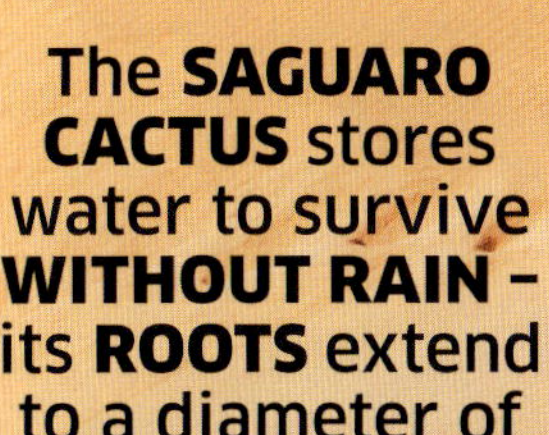

The **SAGUARO CACTUS** stores water to survive **WITHOUT RAIN** – its **ROOTS** extend to a diameter of

30 m
(100ft).

Only **36—41cm** (14–16in) in length, the **FENNEC FOX** has huge **EARS** up to **15cm** (6in) **LONG** to lose **BODY HEAT** and keep cool.

CAMELS can **SURVIVE LOSING** up to **30%** of their **BODY WEIGHT** in **WATER**. (Most mammals would die from **DEHYDRATION** if they lost **12%**.)

GLOBAL WARMING is leading to more **desertification—**dry areas turning into deserts. This problem affects **1—2 BILLION** PEOPLE.

MORE THAN **1/2** of the world's **OIL RESERVES** are under the **ARABIAN DESERT.**

CLIMATE CHANGE causes more frequent **HEATWAVES**: in **2023**, Phoenix, Arizona, in the **Sonoran Desert**, had **31 DAYS** at **43.3°C** (110°F) or more.

The world's **LARGEST SOLAR FARM** is in a **DESERT** in Xinjiang, China. It can generate about **6,090 GIGAWATT HOURS OF ELECTRICITY A YEAR.**

Great
GRASSLANDS

Grasses are among the most important plants on the planet. They grow from the base of their blades, so they can survive being grazed upon by animals. Their success has led to them covering vast treeless areas known by different names around the world – prairies, pampas, steppes, and savannas.

The **GREAT PLAINS** is North America's **LARGEST** grassland, covering **3 million** SQ KM (1,158,000 sq miles) from **CANADA** to **MEXICO**.

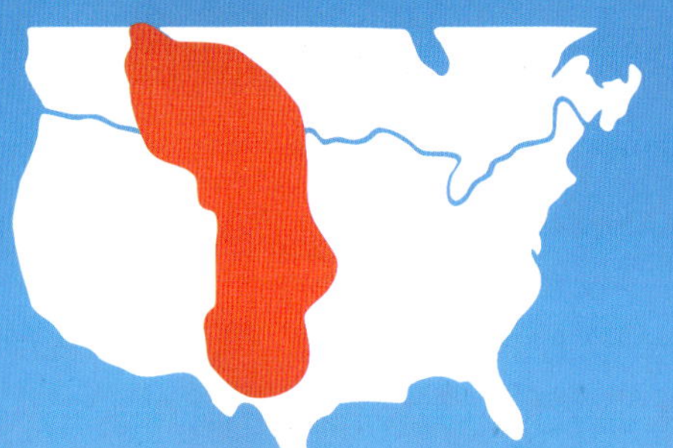

Mongolia has the **LARGEST** area of temperate grassland that's still **INTACT**. At **21,000** SQ KM (8,100 sq miles), it's the size of **EL SALVADOR**.

Grasslands cover between **20** and **40%** of **EARTH'S LAND**.

GRASS makes up **95%** of the **DIET** of the **1.5 million BLUE WILDEBEEST** that migrate across the **AFRICAN SAVANNA.**

The **EURASIAN STEPPE,** the world's **LARGEST TEMPERATE GRASSLAND,** stretches for over **8,000 KM** (5,000 miles), almost **⅓** of the way **AROUND THE WORLD.**

Przewalski's horse

is a **RARE SPECIES** that lives wild on the steppes of **CENTRAL ASIA.** It matches horses painted in caves **17,000 years** ago.

PRAIRIE DOGS live under North American grasslands. Their towns of **TUNNELS** can cover up to **65,000 SQ KM** (25,000 sq miles). The largest town was home to an estimated **400 million ANIMALS.**

More than **99%** of **NORTH AMERICAN PRAIRIE** is used for **AGRICULTURE.**

Until the early **1800s,** up to **60 million bison** lived on the North American plains. Their numbers are now down to about **440,000.**

There are at least **11,500 SPECIES** of grass.

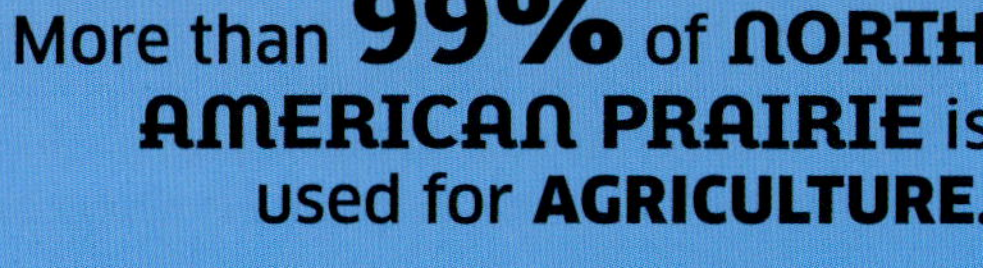

Sweeping
COASTLINES

Forming the border between land and sea, coastlines are our access points to the ocean. There are hundreds of thousands of miles of them on Earth, from sandy beaches to steep cliffs. They are important habitats, shaped by tides, waves, and currents.

Only **1/6** of **EARTH'S coastlines** remain in their **NATURAL STATE** without **HUMAN DEVELOPMENT.**

As much as **90%** of all **MARINE LIFE** is found in **shallow COASTAL WATERS.**

AFRICA has the highest percentage of **SANDY BEACHES** of any continent, with **66%.** **EUROPE** has the lowest at **22%.**

Cliffs are found on **52%** of the **WORLD'S COASTLINE.**

MONACO has the **SHORTEST** coastline of any country that has one – just **5.6 KM** (3.5 miles).

HAWAII'S 1,010 m- (3,313 ft-) **TALL KALAUPAPA CLIFFS** are among the world's **HIGHEST SEA CLIFFS.**

They formed when ⅓ of **MOLOKAI ISLAND** collapsed **1.5 MILLION YEARS AGO.**

Colonies of more than **100,000 seals** can be found on the coasts of **CANADA** and **NAMIBIA.**

There are **4 TYPES** of **BEACH: SANDY, PEBBLE, BOULDER,** and **SHELL.**

The **LONGEST BEACH** is the sandy **PRAIA DO CASSINO, BRAZIL,** which is **254 KM** (158 miles) long.

80% of **WORLDWIDE TOURISM** is in coastal areas.

Grains of sand are **0.0625 — 2 mm** (0.0025–0.08 in) **IN DIAMETER.** Bigger than that is **GRAVEL,** and smaller is **MUD.**

Some **JAPANESE** beaches have **"star sand"** made from the **SHELLS** of **1-CELLED SEA CREATURES** called **foraminifera,** which evolved more than **500 million YEARS AGO.**

44 officially recognized **COUNTRIES** are **landlocked — THEY HAVE NO COAST.**

4 out of **5** of the **WORLD'S** most **POPULATED CITIES** are found on the coast.

There are about **1,500 SPECIES** of **HALOPHYTE (SALT-TOLERANT PLANTS).** They grow mostly in coastal regions on **EVERY CONTINENT** except **ANTARCTICA.**

70 SPECIES of **SEAGRASS** grow in **COASTAL WATERS** around the world.

At **2,027 km** (1,260 miles) in **LENGTH**, the **GREAT BARRIER REEF**, off northeast Australia, is the **LARGEST CORAL REEF** in the world.

The **GREAT BARRIER REEF** is made up of about **2,900 INDIVIDUAL REEFS** and **900 ISLANDS**.

There are **MORE THAN 800** known species of **HARD CORAL**.

The **first CORAL REEFS** emerged on **EARTH** about **548 million** years ago – over **300 million** years before the **DINOSAURS**.

REEFS make up **LESS THAN 0.1%** of the ocean's **SURFACE AREA** but support about **1/4** of **MARINE ANIMAL LIFE**.

Covering **348,700 SQ KM** (133,000 sq miles), the **Great Barrier Reef** is **ALMOST** the size of **GERMANY**.

Some reefs are in the **COLD DEPTHS**. Norway's **RØST REEF** is found **300** to **400 m** (984–1,312ft) **UNDERWATER**.

MOST CORAL REEFS are found in **warm, shallow** water **LESS THAN 50 m** (160ft) **DEEP**.

CORAL REEFS

Though very rare, coral reefs are among the most biodiverse ecosystems on Earth. They provide a home and feeding ground for thousands of marine creatures. Reefs are created by colonies of tiny creatures called polyps, but over time they can grow to be large enough to be seen from space.

The **AREA COVERED** by living coral reefs **DECLINED** by about **50%** between **1957** and **2007** due to **CLIMATE CHANGE** and **OVERFISHING.**

ONCE A YEAR, following a full moon, coral **POLYPS** release **MILLIONS** of **EGGS** and **SPERM** all at the same time on a **SINGLE NIGHT** in a **MASS SPAWNING** event.

Over **4,000 SPECIES** of **FISH** depend on coral reefs.

REEFS are built from the **HARD EXOSKELETONS** of **SOFT-BODIED** creatures called **POLYPS,** which can be as small as **1mm** (0.04in) across, the **SIZE OF A PINHEAD.**

GALÁPAGOS ISLANDS

Named after the once huge population of giant tortoises found there, this island chain in the Pacific is famous for its rich array of habitats and unique animal life. The Galápagos's millions of years of isolation has resulted in some truly unusual creatures, including the marine iguana and the flightless cormorant.

THE GALÁPAGOS are a cluster of **13 ISLANDS** found **1,000 KM** (600 miles) **OFF THE COAST** of **Ecuador,** South America.

The islands were **FORMED** by **VOLCANIC ACTIVITY** and still have **13 active volcanoes.**

Lava cacti are adapted to grow on **FRESH LAVA FIELDS**, and they live exclusively in **11 SPOTS** on **6** of the **GALÁPAGOS ISLANDS.**

The fast-swimming **GALÁPAGOS CORMORANT** has **LOST ITS ABILITY TO FLY.** Its stubby **WINGS** are **1/3** the size they would need to be for **FLIGHT.**

The **GALÁPAGOS'S MARINE IGUANA** is the **1 LIZARD** in the world that **CAN SWIM.**

Naturalist **CHARLES DARWIN** went to the islands in **1835**. The **5-week visit** helped inspire his **theory of evolution.**

THE GALÁPAGOS are located around the **EQUATOR** at the **INTERSECTION** of **3 TECTONIC PLATES** and **5 MAJOR OCEAN CURRENTS.**

The islands boast **3 SPECIES** of **BOOBIES** - with **grey, red,** and **blue** feet!

GIANT TORTOISES can live for up to **1 YEAR** **WITHOUT FOOD OR WATER,** so they almost became extinct due to **SAILORS** keeping them on board for fresh **MEAT.**

This tropical location is home to the **second-smallest penguin**, and the only species found **NORTH** of the **EQUATOR.**

97% of the Galápagos is **PROTECTED** as a **NATIONAL PARK.** Around **30,000** people live on the other **3%.**

The **LARGEST GALÁPAGOS TORTOISE** on record reached **417 KG** (919lb).

The **GALÁPAGOS giant tortoise** is one of the **LONGEST-LIVING LAND VERTEBRATES.** The oldest-known lived to **175.**

The grey-all-over **LAVA GULL** is the world's **RAREST GULL,** with **300—600** individuals, found **ONLY** in the **GALÁPAGOS.**

The **OPEN OCEAN** is Earth's **LARGEST BIOME** by far, with a **VOLUME** of **1.37 billion CUBIC KM** (330 million cubic miles).

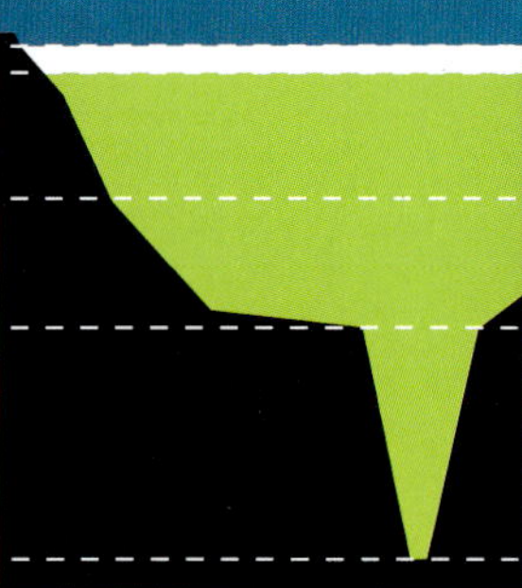

About **90%** of **MARINE LIFE** is found in the **EPIPELAGIC** or **SUNLIGHT ZONE DOWN TO 200m** (650ft).

1 NAUTICAL MILE is **1.15 LAND MILES** or **1.85 KM**. (There is no nautical kilometre.)

FISH travel in **SCHOOLS** across the ocean for **SAFETY IN NUMBERS. Herring** can gather in groups of **HUNDREDS OF MILLIONS,** that stretch for up to **40 KM** (25 miles).

SCIENTISTS estimate that **91%** of **OCEAN SPECIES** are still to be classified.

The **OPEN OCEAN** is home to the **BIGGEST ANIMAL EVER TO HAVE LIVED,** the **BLUE WHALE.** It can reach weights of up to **200 tonnes.**

Many **OCEAN ANIMALS** need to **COME UP FOR AIR** but can dive for minutes to hours at a time. The **LOGGERHEAD TURTLE** can **HOLD ITS BREATH** for up to **10 hours.**

Many marine animals **MIGRATE. GREY WHALES** make the **LONGEST-KNOWN MAMMAL MIGRATION,** making a **19,000 KM** (12,000-mile) **ROUND TRIP** in a **YEAR.**

OPEN OCEAN

The open ocean, also known as the pelagic zone, is the vast area of ocean found away from coasts. The largest biome on Earth, the open ocean is home to tiny plankton, fast-swimming fish, and the largest animals on the planet. Most fishing for human food takes place here too.

The **OCEAN** produces more than **50%** of the **OXYGEN** in the **AIR WE BREATHE**, mostly due to **PLANKTON.**

The **SAILFISH** is the world's **FASTEST FISH**, reaching speeds up to **109 KPH** (68 mph).

WATER PRESSURE increases by about **1 ATMOSPHERE** (pressure at sea level) every **10 m** (32ft) **DEEPER** you go.

There are **NO PLANTS** below **200 m** (655ft) deep in the ocean because there is **NOT ENOUGH LIGHT** for **PHOTOSYNTHESIS.**

SEAWATER contains an average of **3.5% SALT.**

POINT NEMO is the location in the **PACIFIC OCEAN** furthest from land. It is **2,688 km** (1,670 miles) from any **COAST.**

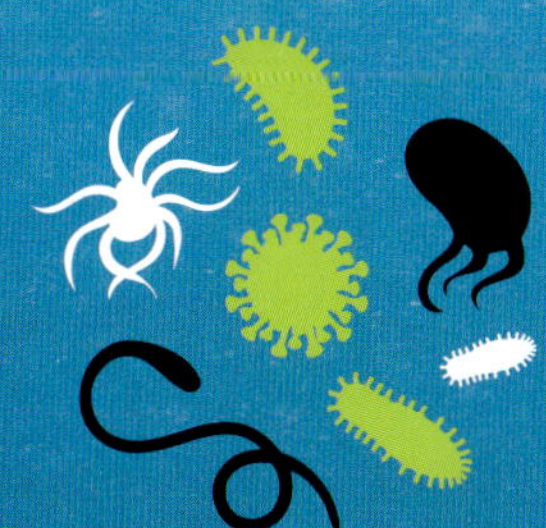

An **AVERAGE LITRE** (about 1 quart) of **seawater** contains over **20,000** kinds of **MICROORGANISM.**

Dark DEEP SEA

Most of the ocean exists in total darkness, and the deeper you go, the higher the pressure due to the weight of all the water above you. Even in these seemingly inhospitable conditions, life has found a way to flourish, with a range of bizarre creatures, many of which can make their own light.

In the ocean's **MIDNIGHT ZONE**, between **1,000** and **4,000 m** (3,280–13,120ft), pressure can reach **630 KG PER SQ CM** (5,850lb per sq in).

The **MIDNIGHT ZONE** has a constant temperature of **4°C** (39°F).

75% of the ocean floor falls in the **ABYSSAL ZONE** between **4,000** and **6,000 m** (13,100–19,700ft).

Most of the ocean is **TOTALLY DARK.** The very furthest sunlight can reach is **1,000 m** (3,280ft) deep.

DEEP-SEA CREATURES live in total darkness, but **3/4** of them make their **OWN LIGHT** through a chemical reaction called **BIOLUMINESCENCE.**

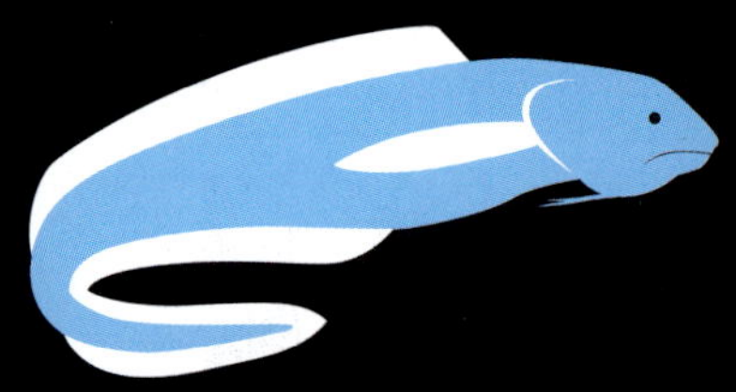

ABYSSOBROTULA GALATHEAE is the **DEEPEST-LIVING FISH** discovered so far. It was found at **8,372 m** (27,467ft) underwater.

The **MARIANA TRENCH,** the very deepest part of the ocean, is **10,994 m** (36,069ft) down.

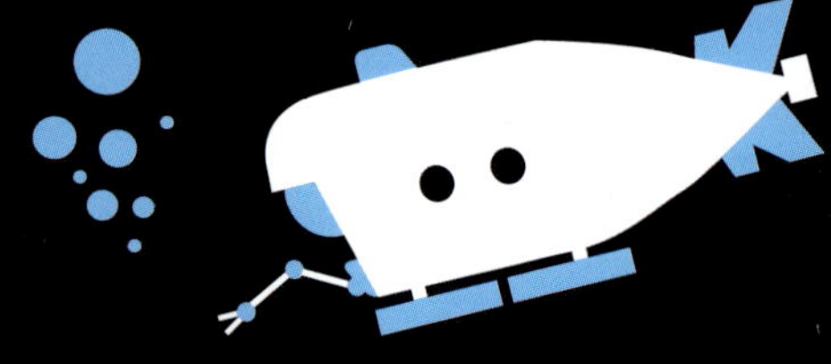

The **PRESSURE** in the **MARIANA TRENCH** is **1,100 TIMES** what humans generally experience on land.

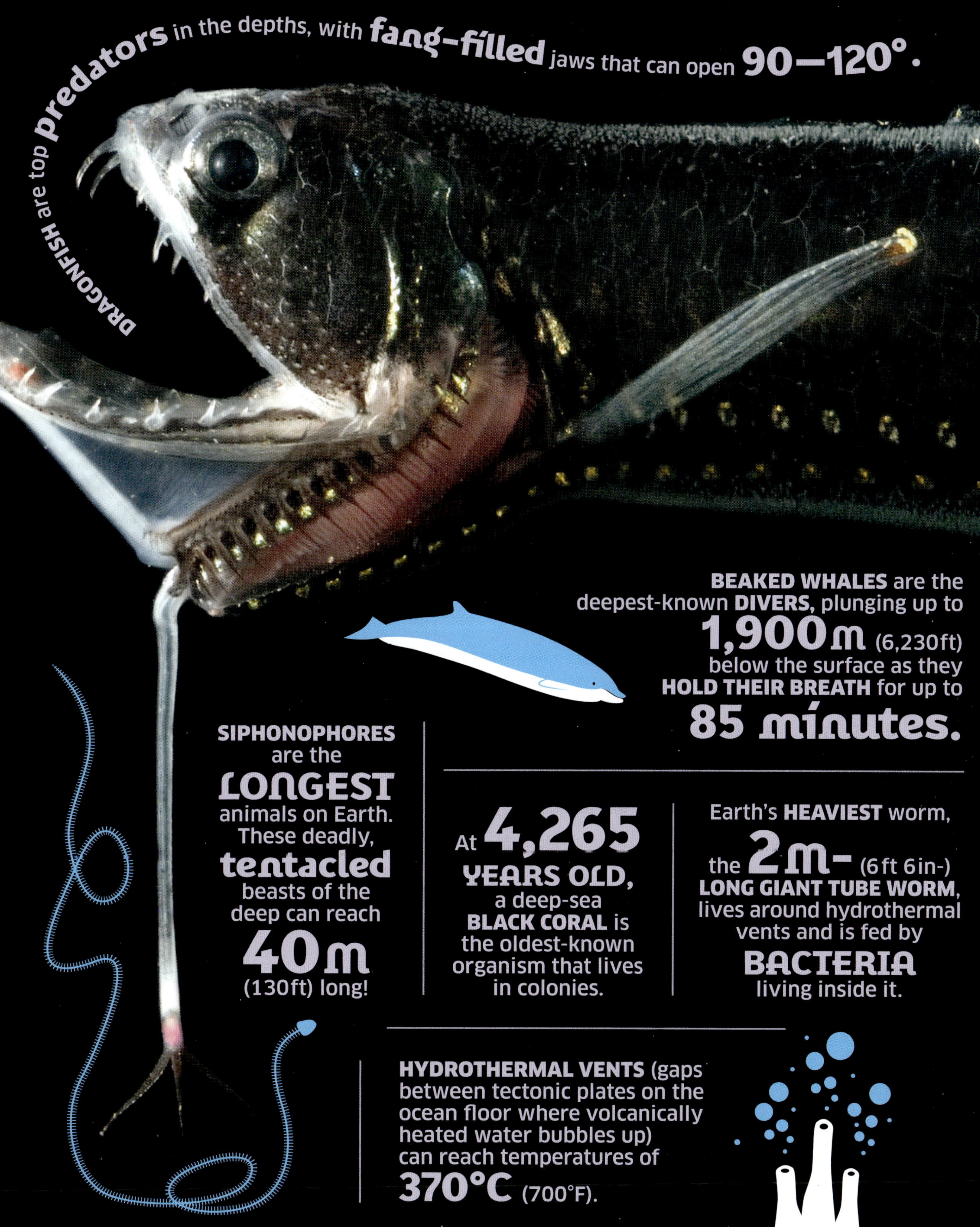

DRAGONFISH are top **predators** in the depths, with **fang-filled** jaws that can open **90–120°**.

BEAKED WHALES are the deepest-known **DIVERS**, plunging up to **1,900 m** (6,230ft) below the surface as they **HOLD THEIR BREATH** for up to **85 minutes.**

SIPHONOPHORES are the **LONGEST** animals on Earth. These deadly, **tentacled** beasts of the deep can reach **40 m** (130ft) long!

At **4,265 YEARS OLD,** a deep-sea **BLACK CORAL** is the oldest-known organism that lives in colonies.

Earth's **HEAVIEST** worm, the **2m-** (6ft 6in-) **LONG GIANT TUBE WORM,** lives around hydrothermal vents and is fed by **BACTERIA** living inside it.

HYDROTHERMAL VENTS (gaps between tectonic plates on the ocean floor where volcanically heated water bubbles up) can reach temperatures of **370°C** (700°F).

HUMAN PLANET

FARMING

Humans began cultivating crops and domesticating animals around 11,000 years ago. Today, farming is a huge industry that helps provide people with food, clothes, and a variety of everyday products. The popular food crop soya beans, for instance, can also be used to make fuel, ink, AstroTurf, and chewing gum.

Sugar cane, which is a type of **GRASS,** is the world's **MOST-PRODUCED** crop, with nearly **2 billion TONNES** harvested **ANNUALLY.**

Around **3.75 MILLION HECTARES** (9 million acres) of **FOREST,** mainly in the tropics, are **CUT DOWN** each year for agricultural use.

Nearly **1/2** of the **WORLD'S INHABITABLE LAND** is used for **FARMING.**

When the **WEIGHT** of **ALL MAMMALS ON EARTH** is added up, **livestock** accounts for **62%** of the total. **WILD ANIMALS** account for only **4%** of mammal biomass, with humans making up the rest.

Around **785 million TONNES** of **WHEAT** are grown annually. **CHINA** produces over ⅙ of that total.

Around **44%** of the **CROPS GROWN** for **HUMANS** are **never eaten.**

There are **500 million SMALL FARMS** around the world.

At least **27%** of the **WORLD'S POPULATION** work in **AGRICULTURE.**

FIGS were one of the **FIRST CROPS. FIG TREES** were grown in modern-day **JORDAN** more than **11,400** YEARS AGO.

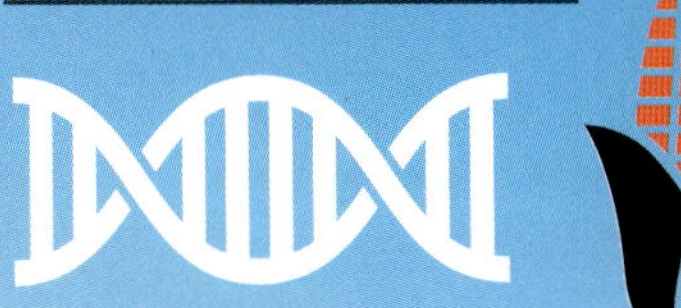

Scientists have created many **GENETICALLY MODIFIED** (GM) crops, usually to make them more **PEST-RESISTANT.**

In the **USA, GM CROPS** account for **92%** of maize, **94%** of soya beans, and **96%** of cotton planted.

3 CROPS — **maize, rice,** and **wheat** — account for **90%** of global **CEREAL FARMING.**

Around **42%** of all the calories that humans around the world eat come from **MAIZE, RICE,** and **WHEAT.**

More **bananas** are **GROWN** and **EATEN** than any other **FRUIT** – at least **115 million** TONNES of them.

CHICKENS are the **MOST FARMED LIVESTOCK.** There are **33 billion** of them in the world, as compared to only **8 billion** PEOPLE.

In **VERTICAL FARMING,** crops are grown **INDOORS** in layered stacks, using water or mist instead of soil. This method can yield **350 times** **MORE** per hectare than conventional farming.

Australia has the **MOST LAND** dedicated to **ORGANIC FARMING** of any country with **353,000** SQ KM (136,300 sq miles).

That's **55%** of all organic farmland in the world.

MINING

Earth has abundant geological resources – materials that are useful to humans but that we cannot grow or make ourselves. These valuable rocks, minerals, and metals can be mined from deep underground, near the surface, or underwater sediments.

SOUTH AFRICA'S MPONENG gold mine is the **DEEPEST** mine in the world at **4 KM** (2.5 miles) **UNDERGROUND.**

The **LARGEST UNDERGROUND COPPER MINE is El Teniente in CHILE** with its **3,000 KM** (1,864 miles) of **DRIFTS (PASSAGES to EXTRACT ORE).**

The **ELEVATOR** down to **MPONENG** travels at **64 KPH** (40mph) and can hold **120 MINERS** at a time.

COAL is the **MOST-MINED** rock on Earth, with an estimated **7.2 billion tonnes** dug up **EACH YEAR.**

The **AVERAGE SMARTPHONE** contains **25 metals** taken from **MINED MINERALS.**

Over **30%** of all the **GOLD** mined globally **since 1886** has come from the **WITWATERSRAND BASIN** of **SOUTH AFRICA**, making this area the largest single source of gold in history.

COPPER was the **FIRST METAL** to be mined. **EGYPTIANS** were mining it as far back as **3000 BCE.**

It takes **2.5 TONNES** of **IRON ORE, COKING COAL,** and **LIMESTONE** to produce **1 TONNE** of **steel.**

Over **1.5 MILLION SQ KM** (580,000 sq miles) of **INTERNATIONAL SEABED** is being set aside for **MINERAL EXPLORATION.**

The **PIT** at **BINGHAM CANYON MINE** in Utah, USA, is the **WIDEST** and **DEEPEST** ever made by humans, stretching **4 KM** (2.5 miles) across and **1.2 KM** (¾ mile) down.

Bingham Canyon Mine is the world's **LARGEST,** employing **2,500 people** to produce **COPPER, GOLD, SILVER,** and **MOLYBDENUM.**

The biggest planned **MINING BLAST** used **8,144 ELECTRONIC DETONATORS** to set off **2,194 tonnes** of **EXPLOSIVES** placed over **3,899 HOLES** at an open-pit coal mine in Australia.

There is estimated to be **50,000 TONNES** of **GOLD RESERVES** underground.

CHINA has more than **40,000 MINES,** 75% of which are underground.

Because **STEEL** is so critical to modern life, humans use **20 times MORE IRON** than **ALL OTHER MINED METALS COMBINED.**

Mined **"AGGREGATES"** (sand, gravel, and crushed rock) make up **80%** of **CONCRETE.**

There is evidence of **HUMAN ANCESTORS** fishing that dates back to **1.95 million years ago** along an ancient lake in **KENYA**.

The **20CM-** (8in-) long **PERUVIAN ANCHOVY** is one of the **MOST FISHED** species. The most caught in one year was **13 million tonnes** in 1971.

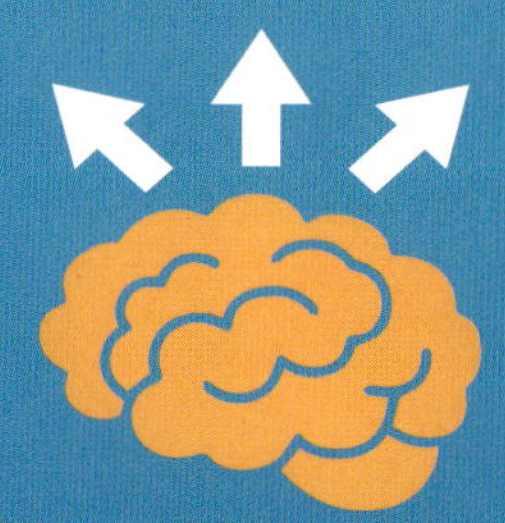

Scientists think eating fish containing **omega-3** and **omega-6** fatty acids, which are **KEY TO HUMAN BRAIN GROWTH**, may have helped our **ANCESTORS** to develop **BIGGER BRAINS**.

In the **US**, **76%** of all seafood consumption comes from only **10 SPECIES**. **SHRIMP** tops the list!

The average inhabitant of **ICELAND** consumes more than **90KG** (200lb) of seafood a year.

More than **10%** of the **GLOBAL POPULATION** relies on fishing for their livelihoods.

The biggest tuna ever caught was **678.6KG** (1,496lb) – that's **4,680** tins of tuna!

This **VIETNAMESE ANCHOVY BOAT** can haul in **10 to 20** batches of **20KG** (44lb) per outing.

FISHING

Humans have caught fish for food since we first evolved. Today, it happens on an industrial scale, and the market for seafood has become one of the largest of any food product. As laws have come in to prevent overfishing, more than half of our seafood now comes from fish farming, or aquaculture.

The **FISHING INDUSTRY** netted a staggering **£528 billion** in 2023.

FARMING accounts for more than **¾ OF SALMON PRODUCTION TODAY,** with around **2.6 million tonnes** farmed in **2023.**

HUMANS now eat around **20.5 KG** (45lb) of **seafood PER PERSON,** more than **DOUBLE** the **GLOBAL AVERAGE** in the **1960s.**

More than **⅓** of **SHARKS** and **RAYS** are threatened with **EXTINCTION** due to **OVERFISHING.**

Illegal fishing accounts for around **20%** of catches.

The **BIGGEST** fishing boat ever built, **ATLANTIC DAWN,** could catch and process **400 tonnes OF FISH** in **24 hours.**

Nearly **7%** of the **PROTEIN** that humans eat comes from fish. In some **COASTAL COMMUNITIES,** that figure is as much as **70%.**

CHINA produces the **MOST SEAFOOD** of any country – more than **70 million tonnes a year.**

It's **LEGAL** to catch **2,200 SPECIES** as seafood. Around **60 TYPES** are **FARMED.**

There are around **5,200 SQ M** (56,000 sq ft) of **FOREST** for **EVERY PERSON** on Earth.

CONIFER TREES are **FELLED** for **TIMBER** after **40 YEARS** of growth.

Around **42%** of wood harvested **each year** goes towards producing **414 million tonnes** of **PAPER PRODUCTS**.

More than **7 million SQ KM** (2.7 million sq miles) of forest grow in **PROTECTED AREAS.**

HARDWOODS such as **MAPLE** and **OAK** take longer to mature. They grow up to **150 YEARS** before harvesting.

A 14 m (45 ft) pine tree provides pulp to make 10,000 sheets of paper.

QUEBRACHO ("axe-breaker") trees of **SOUTH AMERICA** are among the world's **HARDEST,** able to withstand **2 TONNES** (4,570 lb) of force.

Only around **7%** of the world's forests are **planted** rather than **self-seeded.**

More than **50 million TONNES** of **CHARCOAL** are made from wood each year. Around **65%** of that is produced in **AFRICA.**

34% of the world's **CORK-OAK TREES** are in **PORTUGAL,** with the **BARK** used for **BOTTLE CORKS.**

About **496 MILLION CUBIC M** (17 billion cubic ft) of **SAWN WOOD** were produced around the world in **2021.**

FORESTRY

Forests cover nearly 31 per cent of Earth's land and are home to most of the world's land-based plant and animal species. They are also a source of wood, paper, fuel, and medicines. Many forests are carefully managed with fast-growing trees planted and felled. Some forests are protected for recreation or wildlife.

Forests are home to **over 80%** of the world's land-based **ANIMALS, INSECTS,** and **PLANTS.**

Around **50 TYPES** of **SOFTWOOD** and **20,000 TYPES** of **HARDWOOD** are traded **GLOBALLY.**

The **USA** has the **MOST WOOD PLANTATIONS** of any country, with **13 MILLION HECTARES** (32 million acres).

There are about **40.6 million SQ KM** (15.7 million sq miles) of **FOREST** covering the planet.

PAPER can be **RECYCLED 5–7 times.** Recycling 1 TONNE of **PAPER** can save **17 trees.**

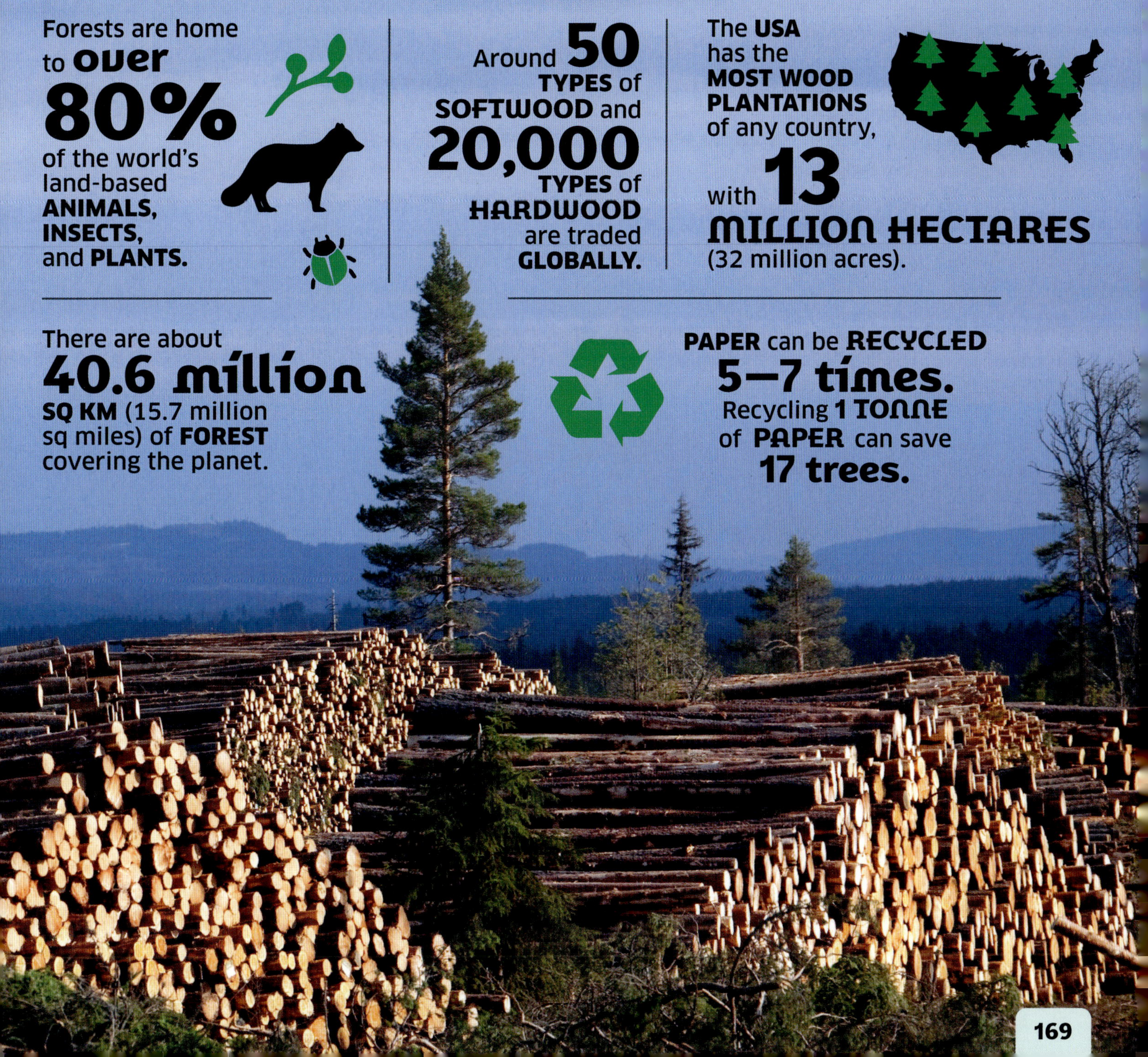

Long-haul
TRANSPORT

Humans became a global species by finding ways to travel and trade by water, land, and air. Today, transportation is a multi-trillion-pound industry responsible for moving billions of tonnes of freight each year.

Around **11 billion** TONNES of goods are shipped by **BOAT ANNUALLY** – that's more than **1 TONNE FOR EVERY PERSON** on **EARTH!**

AUSTRALIA'S SYDNEY HARBOUR is the world's **LARGEST NATURAL PORT**, covering **54 SQ KM** (21 sq miles) and reaching **DEPTHS** of **45m** (148ft).

There are about **1.5 million** PROFESSIONAL SAILORS. More than **25%** of them come from **1 ISLAND** country: the **PHILIPPINES.**

SHANGHAI, CHINA, has the world's **BUSIEST PORT,** shipping more than **49 million** **6m** (20ft) **CONTAINERS A YEAR.**

The **LARGEST** shipping vessels (around 400m / 1310ft long) can carry **18,000+** CONTAINERS – enough to fill a **110 KM-** (68 mile-) long **TRAIN.**

The **TRANS-SIBERIAN RAILWAY** is the **LONGEST** train line. It takes **7 DAYS** to ride it across **8 TIME ZONES.**

There are about **40,000 AIRPORTS** around the world. The **USA** has by far the most with **15,873.**

An average of **102,330 COMMERCIAL FLIGHTS TAKE OFF** each day.

There are around **10,000 PLANES IN THE SKY** at any one time. During the **BUSIEST TIMES,** the number of airborne commercial aircraft can top **20,000.**

Flying with the **POLAR JET STREAM** across the **ATLANTIC** saves planes an average of **30 — 45 MINUTES** on routes from the **US** to **EUROPE.**

Around **11%** of people **fly** each year, including **4% INTERNATIONALLY.**

About **20%** of Earth's land is traversed by **36 million km** (22.4 million miles) of **ROAD,** enough to travel to the **MOON** and **BACK** more than **46 times.**

The **LONGEST ROAD** in the world is the **PAN-AMERICAN HIGHWAY,** which **SPANS** nearly **30,600 km** (19,000 miles) from **ALASKA** to the southern tip of **ARGENTINA.**

AUSTRALIA, with its **LONG, STRAIGHT ROADS** across the **OUTBACK,** has the **LONGEST TRUCKS** – "road trains" up to **49 FT** (160m).

Around **18%** of people **OWN CARS** globally. **NEW ZEALAND** has the highest rate of ownership, with almost **9 CARS** for every **10 PEOPLE.**

During winter, some places have **OFFICIAL ice roads** over frozen water. The **LONGEST** is **475 km** (300 miles), connecting **3 DIAMOND MINES** in Canada.

Statins, which **REDUCE THE RISK** of **HEART ATTACK, STROKE,** or death from **HEART DISEASE** by **25%,** were originally derived from **CHOLESTEROL-LOWERING MOLECULES** found in a **fungus.**

ALEXANDER FLEMING accidentally discovered what is now the most **WIDELY USED ANTIBIOTIC, PENICILLIN,** in 1928, when he found *PENICILLIUM RUBENS* mould growing on a **PETRI DISH OF BACTERIA.**

Today *Penicillium chrysogenum* is used to make the antibiotic penicillin. The mould is grown and **FERMENTED** in huge tanks, which yield **50G** of **PENICILLIN PER LITRE** (1¾oz per quart).

Willow bark was one of the earliest forms of **PAIN** and **FEVER RELIEF,** used up to **4,000 YEARS AGO.**

At least **52,885** species of **FLOWERING PLANT** have **MEDICINAL** uses.

More than **30 million HECTARES** (74 million acres) of land are used to **FARM** medicinal plants in **CHINA.**

The shrub **MADAGASCAR PERIWINKLE** (pictured) can stop cancer cells dividing and is used in chemotherapy medication. The **ACTIVE INGREDIENT** makes up just **0.0003%** of the dry weight of the plant.

MEDICINE

Ancient healing traditions were rooted in nature, but modern medicine still relies heavily on natural sources for many drugs and therapies. Microbes and compounds from plants and fungi are found in everything from cancer treatments to antibiotics.

Between **60** and **80%** of **ALL DRUGS** approved to **TREAT INFECTIONS** and **CANCER** come from **NATURAL SOURCES.**

Over **1/4** of the **DRUGS** used in **MODERN MEDICINE** are made directly from **PLANTS.**

70% **OF THE WORLD'S PLANT SPECIES** with proven **ANTICANCER** properties grow only in **RAINFORESTS.**

Avermectins, drugs developed from **STREPTOMYCES BACTERIA** found in **SOIL,** were first used to **DEWORM PETS** but have since been applied to diseases affecting over **3.4 BILLION PEOPLE.**

The drug **ARTEMISININ,** which has helped treat more than **663 million CASES OF MALARIA,** is derived from the **SWEET WORMWOOD** plant.

In 2016, researchers discovered a powerful new class of **ANTIBIOTIC** (malacidins) after screening the **BACTERIA** found in **2,000 SOIL SAMPLES** sent in by volunteers around the US.

QUININE, first derived from **TREE BARK** in 1820, was used to treat **MALARIA** for **186 YEARS.** The tree it comes from, the **CINCHONA,** is now an **ENDANGERED SPECIES.**

Around **20 APPROVED MEDICATIONS** have their origins in **ocean exploration.** They are derived from chemicals produced by marine animals such as **CORALS, SEA SNAILS,** and **SPONGES.**

The widely used painkiller **CODEINE** is found naturally in **POPPY SAP.** More than **300 tonnes** of it are now produced each year.

Invigorating
ENERGY

Most of our energy comes from fossil fuels, such as coal, oil, and gas. When these fuels are burned, they produce carbon dioxide, a greenhouse gas that warms the atmosphere, leading to climate change. So, many countries are now switching to non-polluting, renewable energy sources, such as the Sun, wind, and water.

About **80%** of the **WORLD'S ENERGY** currently comes from **fossil fuels.**

More than **50%** of every **PIECE OF COAL'S** weight comes from **FOSSILIZED PLANTS.**

The **COAL USED TODAY** began to form about **300 MILLION YEARS AGO,** long before **DINOSAURS** walked on Earth.

About **10%** of the **WORLD'S ELECTRICITY** comes from **NUCLEAR ENERGY,** which is released by the splitting of **ATOMS.**

High-level **NUCLEAR WASTE** can remain **radioactive —** and a danger to life – for up to **1 MILLION YEARS,** so must be **SAFELY STORED.**

The world's **BIGGEST** power plant is **CHINA'S THREE GORGES DAM.** It has the capacity to generate up to **22,500 MEGAWATTS** of electricity, enough to power **3 LARGE CITIES.**

In 2018, **COSTA RICA** used **ONLY RENEWABLE ENERGY** for **300 DAYS IN A ROW,** breaking its own **WORLD RECORD.**

The energy that **THE SUN** sends to Earth in **1 HOUR** is enough to fulfil the world's **ELECTRICITY NEEDS** for **1 YEAR.**

Morocco is home to the world's biggest concentrated **SOLAR FARM** – it's the size of **3,500 FOOTBALL PITCHES.**

Around **745 MILLION PEOPLE** in the world – that's **2 TIMES** the population of the US – don't have access to **ELECTRICITY.**

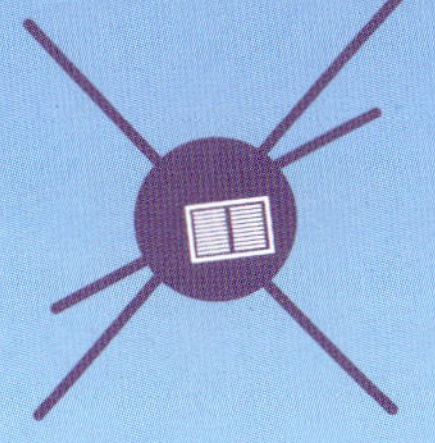

A small **1.5 KG** (3lb) **SATELLITE** called **VANGUARD 1** was the first **SPACECRAFT** to be powered by **solar cells.** Launched in **1958,** it's still orbiting Earth.

32 COUNTRIES have **GEOTHERMAL POWER PLANTS,** which generate energy from the **NATURAL HEAT** Earth produces below its surface.

Just **1 wind turbine** can **GENERATE** enough electricity to power **1,400 HOMES.**

The **ENERGY INDUSTRY** uses more than **2 MILLION KM** (1.25 million miles) of **PIPELINE** to transport gas and oil – almost enough to **CIRCLE THE PLANET 50 times.**

More than **1.5 billion SOLAR PANELS** are manufactured **EACH YEAR.**

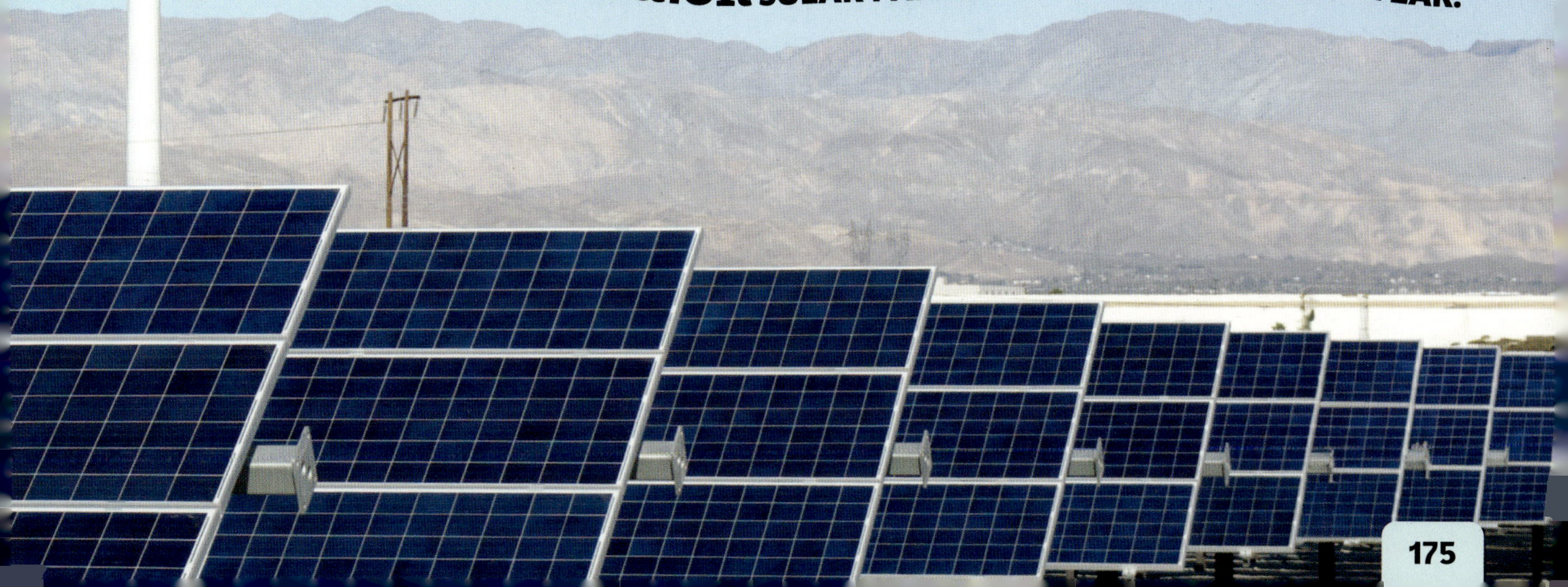

14 of the **top 20** **MOST POPULOUS** urban areas in the world are found in **ASIA.**

HUMANS only make up **0.01%** of the **total biomass** of life **ON EARTH.**

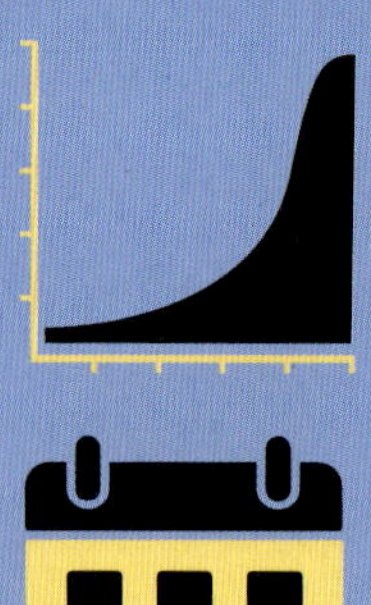

The **RATE** of **POPULATION** growth is slowing. **WORLD POPULATION** is expected to **PEAK** by **2100.**

The **WORLD POPULATION** reached **8 billion** on **15 November 2022.**

Around **110 billion** humans have been born since the **DAWN OF OUR SPECIES,** meaning roughly **7%** **OF ALL PEOPLE** who have ever lived on Earth are **ALIVE TODAY.**

Around **60 MILLION people die every year,** about the equivalent of the population of **SOUTH AFRICA.**

In **1970,** the **WORLD'S POPULATION** was around **1/2** of what it is today.

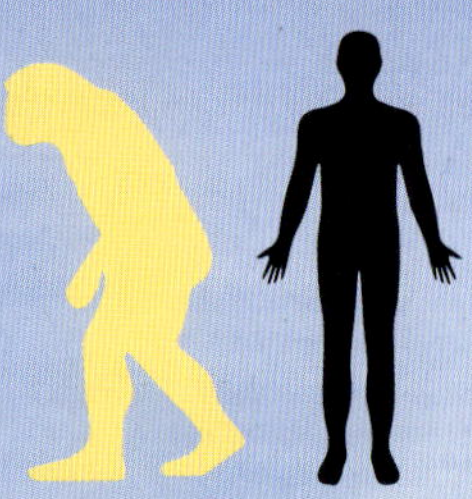

90% of Earth's population lives in the **NORTHERN HEMISPHERE.**

The **USA** has **5%** of **EARTH'S POPULATION** but uses **30%** of its **RESOURCES.**

Over **1/2** of global population growth until **2050** is expected to take place in **AFRICA.**

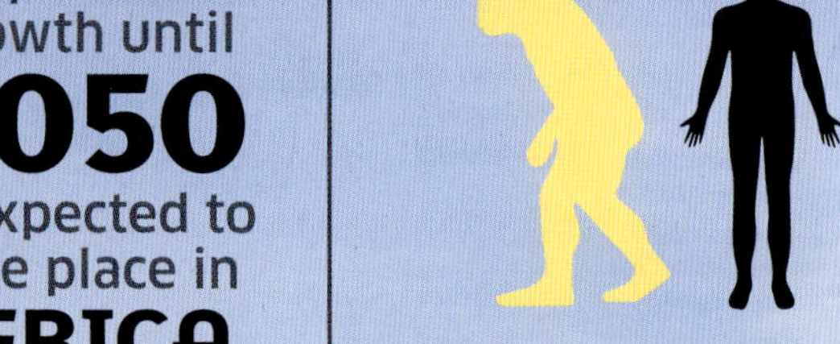

POPULATION

Earth is now home to more than 8 billion humans. People live on every continent, but they are not distributed evenly around the globe. The world's population has grown rapidly over the past century.

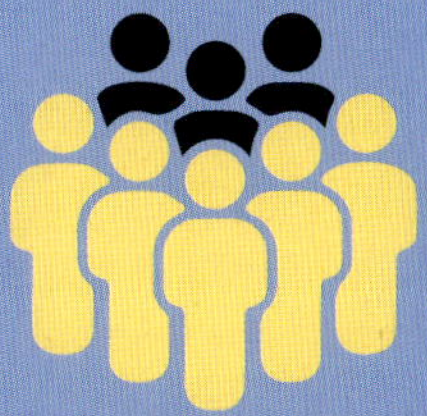

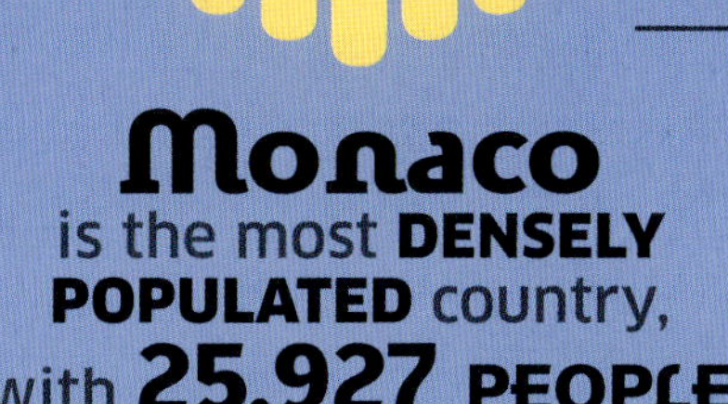

Monaco is the most **DENSELY POPULATED** country, with **25,927 PEOPLE** per sq km (⅖ sq mile).

The **COUNTRY** with the **HIGHEST** population is **INDIA (1.45 BILLION),** closely followed by **CHINA (1.42 BILLION).**

There are about **252 BABIES** born **EVERY MINUTE.**

The **AVERAGE POPULATION DENSITY** across the whole world is around

62 people

PER SQ KM (⅖ sq mile).

GREENLAND is the most sparsely populated country, with just **0.14 PEOPLE PER SQ KM** (⅖ sq mile).

TOP 10
MOST DENSELY POPULATED CITIES (with 1 million+ people)

MANILA • Philippines • Population density: **46,178 PEOPLE PER SQ KM** (119,600 per sq mile)

1

The heart of the world's most densely populated metropolitan area with 16 cities, Manila is the capital of the Philippines. It is a city of skyscrapers and Spanish colonial architecture but up to a third of its residents live in overcrowded slums.

2 **BAGHDAD** • Iraq • Population density: **32,874 PEOPLE PER SQ KM** (85,140 people per sq mile)

Iraq's ancient capital on the Tigris River is home to more than 20 per cent of the country's total population.

3 **MUMBAI** • India • Population density: **32,303 PEOPLE PER SQ KM** (83,660 people per sq mile)

India's financial centre and biggest city (with a population topping 12 million people) is also its most densely populated area.

4 **DHAKA** • Bangladesh • Population density: **29,069 PEOPLE PER SQ KM** (75,290 people per sq mile)

Once the Mughal capital of Bengal, Dhaka is today the modern capital of Bangladesh and a megacity with 10 million+ residents.

5 **CALOOCAN** • Philippines • Population density: **27,989 PEOPLE PER SQ KM** (72,490 people per sq mile)

A growing city and industrial centre in Philippines' Metro Manila area, Caloocan was founded on the island of Luzon in 1762.

6 **PORT-AU-PRINCE** • Haiti • Population density: **27,395 PEOPLE PER SQ KM** (70,950 people per sq mile)

This coastal city, vulnerable to hurricanes and earthquakes, is the capital of the most populous country in the Caribbean.

7 **KARACHI** • Pakistan • Population density: **25,229 PEOPLE PER SQ KM** (65,340 people per sq mile)

Karachi is a port on the Arabian Sea and the biggest city in Pakistan.

8 **KOLKATA** • India • Population density: **24,306 PEOPLE PER SQ KM** (62,950 people per sq mile)

Once the capital of British India, today Kolkata is a major port city on the Hugli River and drives the economy of eastern India.

9 **KATHMANDU** • Nepal • Population density: **23,923 PEOPLE PER SQ KM** (61,960 people per sq mile)

Kathmandu is one of the oldest cities on Earth, founded in the 2nd century in a valley at the base of the Himalayas.

10 **DAMASCUS** • Syria • Population density: **22,221 PEOPLE PER SQ KM** (57,552 people per sq mile)

Besides being the most populous city in Syria, Damascus is the oldest capital city in the world, first settled in the 3rd millennium BCE.

Exciting
CITIES

Cities are built-up densely populated urban areas that are larger or more important than towns. They provide homes and workplaces for many millions of people. Cities can also be the capitals of countries with government offices, business headquarters, skyscrapers, and vast public transport systems.

Around **55%** of the **WORLD'S POPULATION** live in **URBANIZED** areas such as **CITIES**.

Megacities have **10 MILLION+ PEOPLE.** There are **34** of them around the world.

LESS THAN 2% of Earth's **LAND** is made up of **BUILT-UP AREAS,** including cities and towns.

The full **CEREMONIAL NAME** of the **THAI** capital **BANGKOK** is **168 LETTERS LONG** — KRUNG THEP MAHANAKHON AMON RATTANAKOSIN MAHINTHARA AYUTHAYA MAHADILOK PHOP NOPPHARAT RATCHATHANI BURIROM UDOMRATCHANIWET MAHASATHAN AMON PIMAN AWATAN SATHIT SAKKATHATTIYA WITSANUKAM PRASIT.

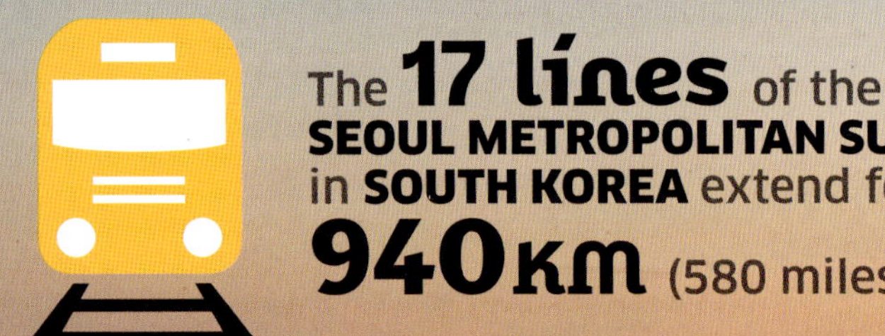

The **17 lines** of the **SEOUL METROPOLITAN SUBWAY** in **SOUTH KOREA** extend for **940 KM** (580 miles).

JERICHO in **PALESTINE** is considered the **OLDEST CONTINUALLY INHABITED** city in the world, at over **11,000 years old.**

The **PACIFIC ISLAND** country of **NAURU** is the only country in the world with

ZERO CITIES.

COASTAL CITIES have added

2,500 SQ KM

(965 sq miles) of **RECLAIMED LAND** to their metropolitan areas since **2020**.

The **MOST POPULOUS** metropolitan area in the world is **TOKYO, JAPAN**. It is home to

37.8 million people,

around **30%** of the country's entire population.

LA PAZ in **BOLIVIA** is the **HIGHEST** capital city in the world, at

3,640 m

(11,942 ft) above sea level, higher than **JAPAN'S MOUNT FUJI**.

The **smallest** CITY in the world is **VATICAN CITY**. It is a **CITY-STATE** that covers less than

0.5 SQ KM

(0.2 sq miles) and is surrounded by the **CITY OF ROME**.

The city of **ISTANBUL** in **TÜRKIYE** spans

2 continents,

EUROPE and **ASIA**.

ISTANBUL, TÜRKIYE, was the **TOP CITY** for international visitors in **2023**, with

20.2 million ARRIVALS.

Tokyo has over **4 times** the population of **New York City**.

14

of the **15 fastest-growing cities** are found in **ASIA**, with **BENGALURU, INDIA**, topping the list.

NEW YORK CITY has around

13,587

licensed **YELLOW TAXI CABS**.

SUPERTREES

In urban Singapore, there is a grove of trees that combine the best of nature and technology into eye-catching sustainable architecture. Gardens by the Bay's "supertrees" were designed to mimic real trees. They're vertical gardens that can harness the Sun's energy, collect rainwater, and release hot, humid air from the nearby greenhouses.

The supertrees are part of a **101-hectare** (250-acre) **GREEN DEVELOPMENT** that also features **2 ENORMOUS CONSERVATORIES.**

There is a **136 m-** (446 ft-) **LONG "SKYWALK"** connecting the trees.

The **CANOPIES** of **11** supertrees have **SOLAR PANELS** that power the park's lights.

The tallest supertree has a **2-STOREY ROOFTOP OBSERVATORY** that can hold **120** people.

GARDENS BY THE BAY has **18** supertrees in **3** clusters.

The **CANOPY** of the supertrees cool the surrounding area and are **30% more efficient** than **TRADITIONAL COOLING SYSTEMS.**

One supertree houses and acts as a chimney for a **30M-** (98ft-) long **BIOMASS BOILER** that can produce up to **7.2 MEGAWATTS** of **POWER** – enough to power **4,000 homes.**

The supertrees act as **VENTS** for the nearby **FLOWER DOME,** keeping this greenhouse at a consistent **25°C** (77°F) and **60%** HUMIDITY, even when it's **37°C** (99°F) outside.

The trunk of each supertree has

3 parts:
A CONCRETE CORE, SURROUNDING STEEL FRAME, and **PLANTING PANELS** that support its **"living bark".**

The boiler burns at least **5,000 tonnes** of **BIOMASS A MONTH,** mixing the ash with the garden's waste to make **FERTILIZER.**

The supertrees host more than **200** species of **PLANTS,** including **FERNS, ORCHIDS,** and **FLOWERING CLIMBERS.**

The **SHORTEST** supertree is **25 m** (80ft) high, and the **TALLEST** is **50 m** (160ft) – around the same height as the **ARC DE TRIOMPHE.**

The supertrees cost **£350 MILLION** to **BUILD.**

GLOSSARY

Agriculture
The practice of farming, including producing crops and raising livestock.

Altitude
The height of an object in relation to the Earth's surface or sea level.

Aquatic
A term used to describe plants and animals that live or grow in water.

Asteroid
A relatively small, rocky object that orbits the Sun.

Atmosphere
The layer of gas that envelops Earth or another planet.

Atoll
A ring-shaped island, or chain of islands, formed of coral that surrounds a lagoon.

Atom
The smallest particle of a chemical element.

Aurora
The appearance of coloured light in the night sky near the poles, caused by electrically charged particles from the Sun interacting with Earth's magnetic field.

Bacteria
A kingdom of microscopic, single-celled organisms found almost everywhere on Earth. Many are helpful, but some cause diseases.

Basalt
A common type of black volcanic rock formed from the rapid cooling of lava.

Biome
An area of the planet that has its own distinctive climate, vegetation, and animal life. Examples include grasslands, forests, and deserts.

Caldera
A large crater formed when a volcano erupts and collapses into its emptied magma chamber.

Calving
The process by which a glacier creates icebergs by shedding blocks of ice into the sea.

Canyon
A rocky valley with steep sides, usually with a river or stream flowing through it.

Carbon dioxide
A colourless gas found in air and absorbed by plants in photosynthesis.

Climate
The general weather conditions in an area over a long period.

Climate change
Long-term changes in temperatures or weather patterns on a global or regional scale.

Conifer
A cone-bearing tree that is typically evergreen with needle-like leaves.

Continent
One of the world's seven large expanses of land (Europe, Asia, Africa, North and South America, Australia, Antarctica).

Continental crust
The part of Earth's crust that forms the continents. It is thicker than oceanic crust.

Coral
The rocklike substance produced by certain marine polyps as hard, external skeletons.

Coral reef
An extensive build-up of corals, generally in warm, shallow seas.

Core
Earth's innermost layer, located beneath the mantle and crust. It consists of a liquid outer core and a solid inner core, both made of nickel and iron.

Crater
A bowl-shaped cavity in the ground, typically caused by an explosion or a meteorite impact.

Crust
The outermost layer of Earth, consisting of the continental crust and oceanic crust.

Crystal
A solid material with an orderly internal atomic structure and flat external faces.

Cumulonimbus
A tall and dense storm cloud that produces heavy rain, lightning, and hail.

Cyclone
A system of winds rotating around a strong centre of low atmospheric pressure. Tropical cyclones are also known as hurricanes and typhoons.

Deciduous
A tree or shrub that shreds its leaves

annually, usually in autumn.

Delta
An area of land where a river divides into several smaller rivers before entering the sea.

Density
The mass of an object or substance divided by its volume. High density denotes a high degree of compactness.

Dormant
A dormant volcano is one that has the potential to erupt but is not currently erupting.

Earthquake
A sudden, violent shaking of Earth's surface caused by movements within the Earth's crust or volcanic action.

Ecosystem
A community of organisms and their environment. Examples include a pond or a rainforest.

Element
A simple substance made of atoms that are all of the same kind. It cannot be broken down into any other substance.

Elevation
The height of an object above sea level or ground level.

Emission
The production or release of something (such as gas or heat) from a source.

Epicentre
The part of Earth's surface directly above the focus of an earthquake. The effects of an earthquake are felt most strongly here.

Equator
An imaginary line running around Earth's circumference that divides it into Northern and Southern hemispheres and marks the zero of latitude.

Erosion
The gradual wearing away of the Earth's surface by water, wind, or other natural agents.

Estuary
The widened mouth of a river where it meets the ocean and tidal action mixes fresh and salt water.

Evergreen
A tree or bush that retains its leaves all year round.

Evolution
The process by which living organisms change and develop over many generations.

Extinction
The disappearance of a species.

Fault
A fracture in the rocks of Earth's crust. Slabs of rock can move past each other at a fault, which can lead to earthquakes.

Flash flood
A sudden and severe flood, typically caused by heavy rain.

Floodplain
A flat area of land next to a river or other waterway that is prone to flooding.

Fossil
The preserved remains or traces of a once-living organism. Fossils offer insights into past life.

Fossil fuel
An energy source formed naturally in the Earth's crust from decayed organic material. Fossil fuels are non-renewable, meaning their supply is limited. Examples include oil, gas, and coal.

Fungi
A kingdom of organisms that produces spores and feeds on organic matter. Some types of fungus are poisonous or cause disease.

Galaxy
A system of millions or billions of stars, gas, and dust held together by gravity.

Gemstone
An attractive precious or semi-precious stone, often used to make jewellery.

Geothermal
Heat generated within Earth. Geothermal energy is a form of renewable energy.

Geyser
A hole in the ground from which hot water and steam burst out with great force.

Glacier
A large mass of ice, formed from compressed snow, that moves slowly.

Gravity
The force of attraction between all bodies of matter. On Earth, it pulls objects towards the centre of the planet.

Greenhouse gas
A gas in the atmosphere that traps heat, contributing to the greenhouse effect (warming of Earth).

Habitat
The environment where an animal or plant naturally lives.

Hurricane
A violent tropical storm with winds of at least 119kph (74mph).

Ice age
A long period with very cold global temperatures and widespread glaciers.

Ice sheet
A mass of glacial ice greater than 50,000 sq km (20,000 sq miles).

Iceberg
A large mass of ice that has broken off from a glacier or ice sheet and floats in the sea.

Igneous rock
A type of rock formed by the cooling and solidifying of magma or lava.

Invertebrate
An animal that lacks a backbone, such as an insect or mollusc.

Jet stream
A narrow current of strong winds that move from west to east high in the atmosphere.

Latitude
The distance of a place north or south of the Equator, expressed in degrees.

Lava
Molten rock that flows from a volcano or other opening in the surface of Earth.

Lithosphere
The solid, outer part of Earth, consisting of the crust and upper mantle.

Magma
Hot liquid rock found below Earth's surface.

Magnetic field
The area around a magnetic body, such as Earth, where magnetic force is exerted.

Mammal
A warm-blooded vertebrate animal that produces milk to feed its young.

Mantle
The thickest layer of Earth that lies between the crust and the core. It is made of rocks that move very slowly.

Mesosphere
The layer of Earth's atmosphere between the stratosphere and the thermosphere.

Metamorphic rock
A type of rock that has undergone a transformation due to intense heat and/or pressure.

Meteor
A piece of rock or metal from space that burns very brightly as it travels through Earth's atmosphere.

Meteorite
A piece of rock or metal from space that has landed on Earth.

Meteoroid
A space rock under 1m (3ft) in diameter.

Methane
A colourless, odourless, greenhouse gas that is the main constituent of natural gas, which is often used as a fuel.

Microorganism
A lifeform, such as a bacterium or fungus, that is so tiny it can only be seen through a microscope. Also known as a microbe.

Mid-ocean ridge
An underwater volcanic mountain chain formed at the boundary between two tectonic plates that are moving apart from one another.

Migration
The act of moving from one region to another. Some animals migrate on a seasonal basis, in search of breeding grounds, food, water, or better conditions.

Mineral
A solid, inorganic substance that is naturally present on Earth.

Mohs scale
A scale that measures the relative hardness of minerals and materials by their resistance to scratching. The scale goes from one to 10, with 10 representing the hardest.

Molecule
The smallest particle of a substance that retains all the properties of the substance. Molecules consist of two or more atoms that are chemically bonded together.

Molten
An object that has been liquified by heat.

Moon
An object that orbits a planet or another celestial body that is not a star.

Native element
A naturally occurring element that is uncombined with other elements.

Nuclear energy
A low-carbon form of energy released from the nucleus, or core, of an atom.

Orbit
The curved path through which objects in space move around a celestial body that has gravity.

Ore
A substance found in the ground from which metals or other valuable minerals can be extracted.

Organism
Any living thing that functions as an individual, such as an animal or plant.

Oxygen
A colourless, odourless gas that makes up about 20% of Earth's atmosphere.

Photosynthesis
The chemical process by which plants, algae, and some bacteria use sunlight, carbon dioxide, and water to make nutrients.

Plankton
Tiny organisms that live and drift in water.

Plateau
A wide area of elevated land with steep sides but a flat top.

Pollutant
A substance that has an adverse effect on land, water, air, or living organisms.

Precipitation
Water that collects in the atmosphere and falls back to Earth, especially as rain or snow.

Rift
A place where Earth's lithosphere is being pulled apart.

Sediment
A solid material that has been broken down by processes of weathering and erosion, and moved to a new location.

Sedimentary rock
A layered rock that is formed from deposits of pre-existing rocks or the remains of once-living organisms.

Seismic
Relating to or caused by an earthquake or vibration of Earth.

Silicate
A mineral composed of silicon, oxygen, and one or more other elements. Silicates are found in many rocks.

Solar system
A gravitationally bound system of planets and other bodies that revolve around a star.

Solar wind
The continual stream of electrically charged particles released from the Sun.

Species
A group of organisms that share common features and are capable of interbreeding.

Stalactite
An icicle-shaped formation that hangs from the roof of a cave and is formed by the trickling of mineral-rich water.

Stalagmite
A type of rock formation rising from a cave floor that is formed by mineral-rich water trickling from the cave's roof.

Star
A large, self-luminous mass of hot gas that radiates energy and is held together by its own gravity.

Tectonic plate
One of the gigantic fragments of Earth's lithosphere that move slowly and constantly in relation to each other.

Temperate
A region or climate characterized by moderate or mild temperatures.

Tidal bore
A large wave that travels upstream in a river or an estuary, against the current.

Tropics
The hottest regions of Earth that lie close to the Equator.

Tsunami
A series of giant waves caused by disturbances, such as an undersea earthquake, volcanic eruption, or landslide.

INDEX

ACKNOWLEDGMENTS

The publisher would like to thank the following people for their help in the making of this book:
Annie Arnold and Matthew Taylor for design; Cath Senker, Kate Shear, and Sara Stanford for writing; Jo Penning for the index; Nick Funnell for proofreading; Claire Lister for editing; Laura Barwick for picture research; and Philip Eales for fact-checking.

Picture Credits

The publisher would like to thank the following for their kind permission to reproduce their photographs:

(Key: a-above; b-below/bottom; c-centre; l-left; r-right; t-top)

4 Getty Images / iStock: Elizabeth M. Ruggiero (tr). **Getty Images:** Jim Sugar (cr). **NASA:** (ftr). **5 Alamy Stock Photo:** Roland Nagy (cr). **naturepl.com:** Stefan Huwiler (cl); Steven David Miller (tl); Donald M. Jones / Minden (tr). **6 Alamy Stock Photo:** Zoonar GmbH (br). **Science Photo Library:** Sebastian Kaulitzki (cra). **Shutterstock.com:** Andrew Buckin (bl). **7 Alamy Stock Photo:** Roland Nagy (br). **naturepl.com:** Suzi Eszterhas (bl); Wild Wonders of Europe / Lundgre (cla). **Science Photo Library:** Reed Timmer (tr). **9 Getty Images / iStock:** Elizabeth M. Ruggiero (stars). **NASA:** (c). **10-11 NASA. 12-13 Getty Images:** adventtr (Earth and Sun). **Getty Images / iStock:** Elizabeth M. Ruggiero (stars). **12-13 NASA** (planets). **14-15 Science Photo Library:** Mark Garlick. **16 Science Photo Library:** Sebastian Kaulitzki. **19 Getty Images / iStock:** 24K-Production. **20-21 Getty Images:** Nick Fitzhardinge. **22-23 Alamy Stock Photo:** dotted zebra. **24-25 Science Photo Library:** Detlev van Ravenswaay. **27 Getty Images:** Jim Sugar. **29 Dorling Kindersley:** Satellite Imagemap / Planetary Visions. **31 naturepl.com:** Wild Wonders of Europe / Lundgre. **32-33 naturepl.com:** Jack Dykinga. **34-35 Getty Images / iStock:** montgomerygilchrist. **36-37 Getty Images:** DEA / ALBERT CEOLAN / Contributor. **38-39 Getty Images:** Paul Souders. **40-41 Getty Images /**

iStock: aphotostory. **42-43 Alamy Stock Photo:** ADS. **44-45 naturepl.com:** Suzi Eszterhas. **46-47 Getty Images:** Liu Jin / AFP. **48-49 Getty Images / iStock:** DanielPrudek. **50-51 Alamy Stock Photo:** Giulio Ercolani. **52-53 Getty Images:** Mike Rowbottom. **54-55 Getty Images:** Nico De Pasquale Photography. **56-57 Getty Images:** Laurie Noble. **58-59 Shutterstock.com:** Mia2you. **60-61 Alamy Stock Photo:** Westend61 GmbH. **62-63 Getty Images:** shayes17. **64-65 Alamy Stock Photo:** Lanmas. **66-67 Getty Images:** Walter Bibikow. **68-69 Dreamstime.com:** Mirecca. **70-71 Getty Images:** ElementalImaging. **72-73 Shutterstock.com:** Sebastian Janicki. **Wikipedia:** Kent G. Budge (background). **75 naturepl.com:** Steven David Miller. **76-77 naturepl.com:** Steven David Miller. **78-79 Florian Ledoux Photography**. **80-81 Getty Images:** Guang Cao. **82-83 Alamy Stock Photo:** LWM / NASA / LANDSAT. **84-85 Getty Images:** Jami Tarris. **86-87 Alamy Stock Photo:** Zoonar GmbH. **88-89 Getty Images:** inigoarza. **90-91 Dreamstime.com:** Kelly Headrick. **92-93 Getty Images / iStock:** leonid_tit. **94-95 Getty Images:** Craig Hastings. **96-97 Getty Images:** Edwin Remsberg. **98-99 Alamy Stock Photo:** Arterra Picture Library. **100-101 Getty Images:** Liz Leyden. **103 naturepl.com:** Stefan Huwiler. **104-105 naturepl.com:** Stefan Huwiler. **106-107 Getty Images:** sharply_done. **Science Photo Library:** Sebastian Kaulitzki (t). **108-109 Getty Images:** Nick Brundle Photography. **110-111 Alamy Stock Photo:** Stocktrek Images, Inc.. **112-113 Getty Images:** Sirachai Arunrugstichai. **114-115 Science Photo Library:** Reed Timmer. **116-117 Getty Images:** Jure Batagelj / 500px. **118-119 Alamy Stock Photo:** mauritius images GmbH. **120-121 Getty Images:** Heath Korvola. **122-123 Getty Images:** Sadik Demiroz. **124-125 naturepl.com:** Pascal Tordeux. **126-127 Getty Images:** Jadwiga Figula. **128-129 Getty Images:** Andrew Merry. **130-131 Getty Images:** Paul Souders. **133 naturepl.com:** Donald M. Jones /

Minden. **134-135 naturepl.com:** Donald M. Jones / Minden. **136-137 Alamy Stock Photo:** Jarmo Piironen. **138-139 Getty Images:** DenisTangneyJr. **140-141 Shutterstock.com:** Al'fred. **142-143 Dreamstime.com:** Samystclair. **144-145 naturepl.com:** Tim Fitzharris / Minden. **146-147 Getty Images:** Martin Harvey. **148-149 Alamy Stock Photo:** Tuul and Bruno Morandi. **150-151 Getty Images:** Francesco Vaninetti Photo. **152-153 Getty Images:** cinoby. **154-155 naturepl.com:** Tui De Roy. **156-157 Getty Images:** Stuart Westmorland. **159 naturepl.com:** David Shale. **161 Alamy Stock Photo:** Roland Nagy. **162-163 Shutterstock.com:** Aleksandr Rybalko. **164-165 Dreamstime.com:** Juan Antonio Barros Moreno. **166-167 Getty Images:** Tan Dao Duy. **168-169 Alamy Stock Photo:** Arterra Picture Library. **170-171 Dreamstime.com:** Pipat Wongsawang. **172-173 Alamy Stock Photo:** Chatchai Somwat. **174-175 Science Photo Library:** GIPHOTOSTOCK. **176-177 Getty Images:** Jason Edwards. **178-179 Getty Images:** Nikada. **180-181 Alamy Stock Photo:** Roland Nagy. **182-183 Alamy Stock Photo:** Sean Pavone

Cover images: Front: 123RF.com: leonello calvetti tc; **Dreamstime.com:** Corey A Ford cla, Konstantinpetkov cra; **Getty Images:** shayes17 br; **Getty Images / iStock:** vlad61 bl; **Back: Shutterstock.com:** Sebastian Janicki clb, Aleksandr Rybalko br; **Spine: Getty Images:** shayes17 t

All other images © Dorling Kindersley
For further information see:
www.dkimages.com

Our WORLD in NUMBERS

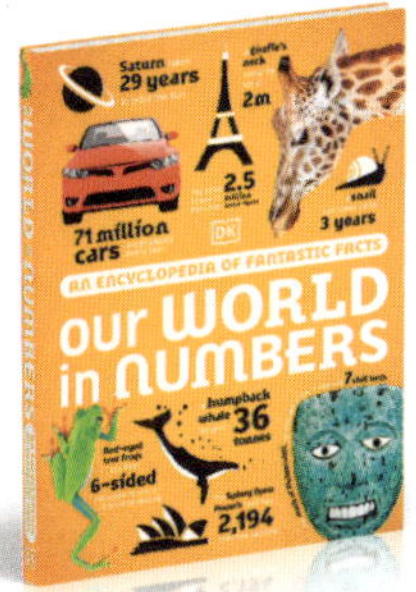 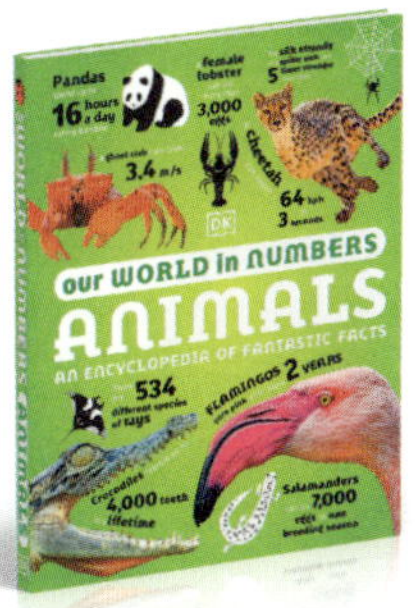  

Our WORLD in PICTURES

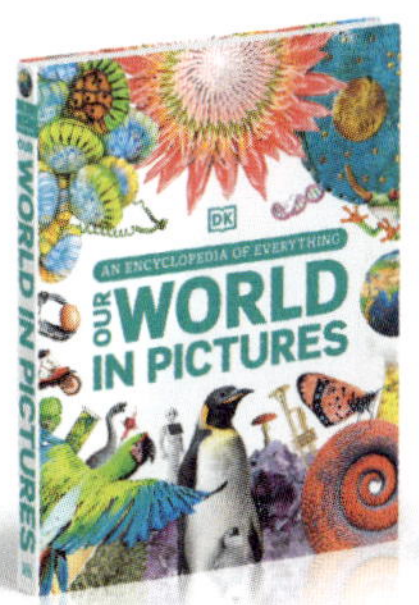 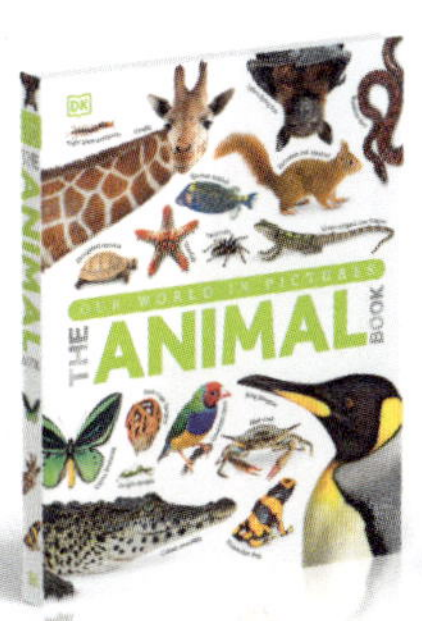 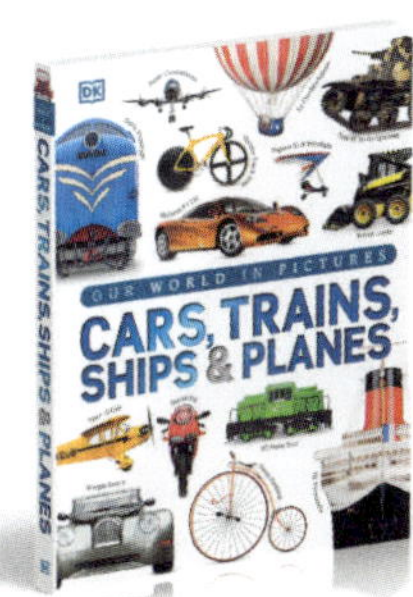 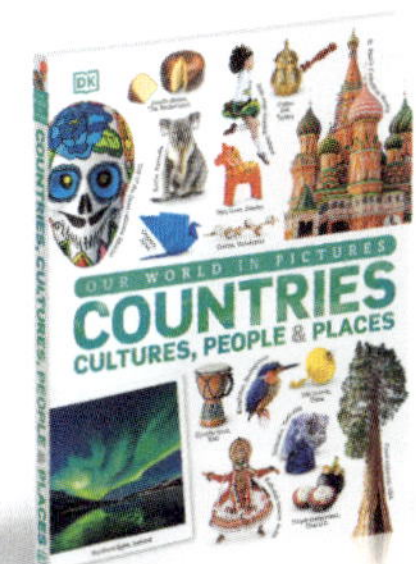

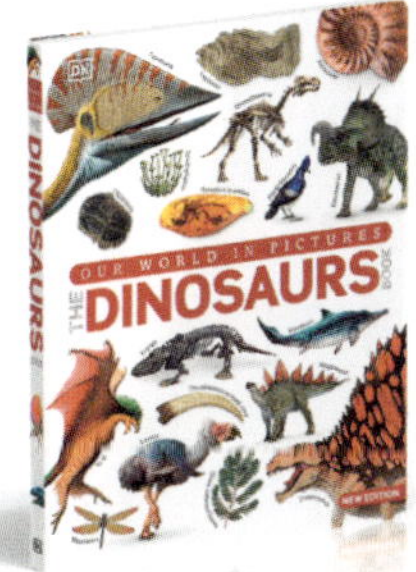 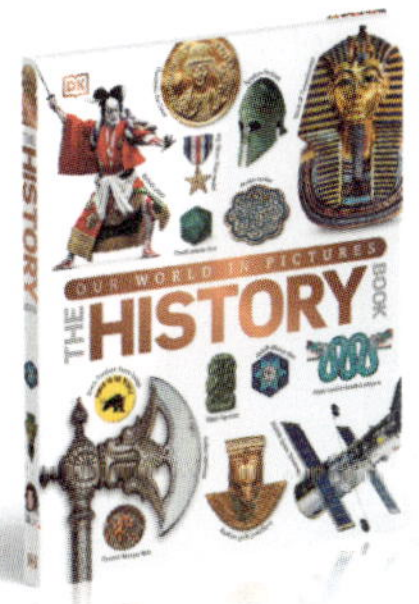 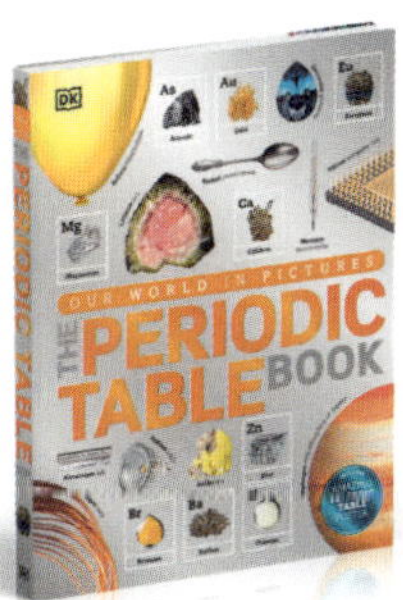  

FLASH CARDS

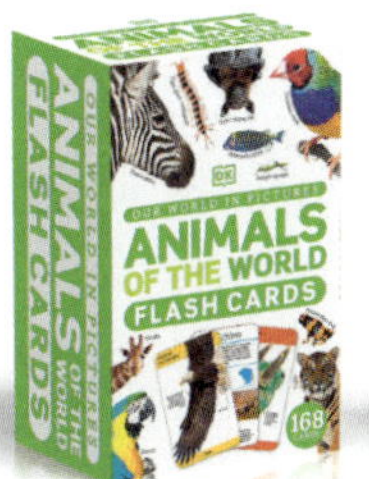  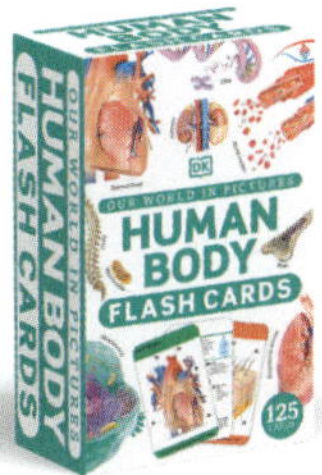 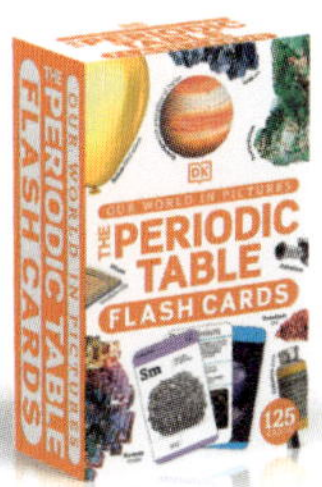 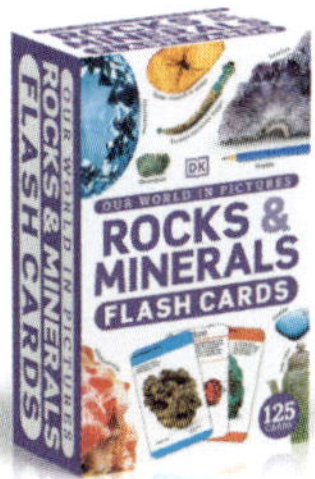